A Symphony of New Testament Hymns

Commentary on

Philippians 2:5-11, Colossians 1:15-20,
Ephesians 2:14-16, 1 Timothy 3:16,
Titus 3:4-7, 1 Peter 3:18-22,
and 2 Timothy 2:11-13

ROBERT J. KARRIS, O.F.M.

D1444399

A Liturgical Press Book

THE LITURGICAL PRESS
Collegeville, Minnesota

227.06
Ka s

Cover design by Greg Becker

Excerpts are taken from the New American Bible, © 1991, 1986, 1970, by the Confraternity of Christian Doctrine, 3211 Fourth Street N.E., Washington, DC 20017-1194, and from the New Revised Standard Version Bible, Catholic edition, © 1989 by the Division of Christian Education of the National Council of Churches of Christ in the USA. Used by permission. All rights reserved.

1   2   3   4   5   6   7   8

Library of Congress Cataloging-in-Publication Data

Karris, Robert J.
   A symphony of New Testament hymns : commentary on
  Philippians 2:5-11 . . . / Robert J. Karris.
      p.   cm.
  Includes bibliographical references.
  ISBN 0-8146-2425-1
  1. Bible N.T. Epistles—Criticism, interpretation, etc.
  2. Hymns—History and criticism. 3. Jesus Christ—History of
doctrines—Early church, ca. 30–600. I. Title.
BS2635.2.K37   1996
227'.06—dc20   96-25645
                                            CIP

For the provincial and custodial ministers
of the O.F.M. English Speaking Conference

Contents

I. INTRODUCTION

Why a book on New Testament hymns? I draw my inspiration in part from my desire to make available, in a popular and faith-filled way, some of the research conducted over the last seventy years into the Christological hymns. Just as certain contemporary artists, e.g., The Baltimore Consort, retrieve ancient songs like the "Early Music of Scotland," I want to revive for our contemporary enjoyment and the deepening of our faith some of the songs which were on the top ten list of the New Testament's Billboard of Hymns. It is my conviction that we have much to learn from what these songs proclaimed about Jesus Christ at a time when the four Gospels had not yet been published.

In arranging my analyses of the New Testament hymns, I have also drawn inspiration from American composer Roy Harris' Fourth Symphony, also called his *Folksong Symphony*. In composing this symphony during the early part of World War II, Harris drew from the treasury of American traditional folksongs and arranged the hymns in such a way as to play upon deep and universal emotions: love ("The Girl I Left Behind Me"); fear of dying and being buried away from loved ones ("Oh Bury Me Not On The Lone Prairie"); hope of returning after battle to a warm homecoming ("When Johnny Comes Marching Home"). Harris could have selected other traditional hymns and arranged them differently, but he created what he did to speak to his country's needs in the early 1940s. While each one of the folksongs had a meaning in its own right, that meaning took on additional coloring by being set within the context of the entire symphony at a critical point in American history.

In my own way, I select and arrange some "traditional" New Testament, pre-60 C.E. hymns to speak to our circumstances. While these hymns have definite meanings within the context of their own writings and also had meaning when they existed outside these writings, they will take on added meaning by being set next to one another in the Karris Symphony.

After chapters on beginnings and background I start my symphony proper with the hymn of Philippians 2:6-11, which draws upon the deep Christian and human experience of humiliation and hope of vindication as it sings about Jesus' self-sacrifice and vindication by God. My second hymn is Colossians 1:15-20 and its cosmic Christology, so much needed today in our dealings with ecological and other world-embracing issues. There is so much need today for reconciling peoples, North and South, male and female. So the third movement of my symphony concentrates on Ephesians 2:14-16 and 1 Timothy 3:16. My fourth movement has baptism as its theme. The hymns of Titus 3:4-7 and 1 Peter 3:18-22 will hopefully broaden the Christian understanding of baptism, perhaps one-sidedly dependent upon the Paul of Romans. My interpretations can be used with great benefit in programs dealing with the Roman Catholic Rite of Christian Initiation of Adults (RCIA). Finding precedent in certain mavericks of the symphonic tradition, I write a fifth movement dealing with the last things. What's it going to be like up yonder? 2 Timothy 2:11-13 will give us a vision of the future and affirm us in our hopes. This symphonic material can be useful at wakes and funerals, in dealings with persons who are concerned about the Rapture, and in our own personal reflections about what's in store for those who have died with Christ in baptism. A concluding chapter will give a retrospective look at the many Christological themes which have sounded through the five movements of the Karris Symphony.

As I consider these New Testament hymns and address some contemporary issues of faith, it might be that my readers will take a clue from the arrangements of Harris and Karris and rearrange these hymns into a new symphonic form to speak to their own situations of challenge and hope, perhaps taking the shorter movements first and then working into the longer ones.

My format for each chapter is simple: (1) presentation of the New Testament hymn and analysis of its structure, (2) setting of context, (3) analysis of the key concepts and images of the hymn, (4) reflection starters on the contemporary significance of the hymn, and (5) annotated bibliography.

I conclude the book with an apology and a sales pitch. I am sorry to say that I do not treat each and every New Testament hymn. Conspicuous by its absence from my symphony is the hymn in the prologue of John's Gospel. Also untreated in my book—except for a cameo appearance of Mary's *Magnificat* in chapter one—are the four canticles or hymns in Luke's infancy narrative. But as there are so many excellent and accessible renditions of these hymns and so few about the seven in my symphony, I feel justified in concentrating primarily on hymns in the Pauline tradition. Perhaps in my next symphony I will draw inspiration from John's prologue, Luke's four canticles, Romans 1:3-4, 2 Corinthians 5:17-21, Hebrews 1:3-4, Revelation 5:9-14, and other material in the New Testament currently being proposed as hymnic.

What audiences do I have in mind for my book? On the academic level, my book can profitably be used as a supplementary text for introductory courses on the New Testament, for I devote a considerable amount of attention to the basic tools and methods needed to interpret the New Testament. Also, courses on Paul's writings may find in my symphony a useful text on letters which are a little out of the Pauline mainstream of Romans, 1 and 2 Corinthians, Galatians, Philippians, 1 Thessalonians, and Philemon. To further these two possible academic uses of my text, I have added an annotated bibliography at the conclusion of most chapters.

For those looking for a book of biblical spirituality, this is a book for you, for it is written brightly and respectfully by a scholar who wears his learning lightly. Behind the five-step format of each chapter is my adaptation of the traditional *lectio divina* approach to the Bible: The text is closely read, with reference to the Greek text when necessary. Meditation follows attentive reading. After probing the meaning of the text by meditation, the One about whom the text sings is contemplated. Finally, general suggestions are offered regarding how readers might turn reading, meditation, and contemplation into praxis.

Finally, liturgists and musicians will find a source of inspiration in the New Testament hymns and their arrangements in the Karris Symphony.

At the end of this Introduction I take the opportunity to commence a list of Thank Yous. I am especially grateful to two people who warmly applauded the Karris Symphony when its first notes were written and who have continued to clap their hands as all five movements have taken shape: Lyn Osiek in Chicago and Peter Williams in Rome. The library at Catholic Theological Union at Chicago has provided a feast of New Testament books for this itinerant author, and CTU's library staff has always been ready to help me find a hymn or two. Robert Hutmacher, J. Michael Thompson, Mary Catherine Keene, Jeannette Scholer, musicians one and all, have offered much encouragement. During a January 1996 course on the material of this book at The Franciscan School of Theology in Berkeley, my students saved me from some faulty notations and joyfully joined me in an exploration of the power of God's word in hymnic form. I thank them for the marvelous experience we all had of how academic study feeds into and in turn is nourished by prayerful reflection upon God's word. Finally, I thank all, who in one way or another, have contributed to the lines and notes which constitute the Karris Symphony. I alone, however, am responsible for any unplayable or sour notes which may remain.

I dedicate my First Symphony to the provincial and custodial ministers of the O.F.M. English Speaking Conference of North America, England, Ireland, and Malta, with whom I have had the pleasure of being associated since 1987. I single out three for special mention because they have been and continue to be an inspiration and example to me of how to combine the vocations of scholar and administrator—Anthony Carrozzo, Joseph Chinnici, and Donald MacDonald.

II. CHAPTER 1

Beginnings

I don't mind who writes the theological books, so long as I can write the hymns.

—Ralph P. Martin, *Worship in the Early Church*

Before the message there must be the vision,
Before the sermon the hymn,
Before the prose the poem.

—Amos N. Wilder, *Theopoetic*

And I (Job) used to have six psalms and a ten-stringed lyre. I would rouse myself daily after the feeding of the widows, take the lyre, and play for them. And they would chant hymns. And with the psaltery I would remind them of God so that they might glorify the Lord.

—Testament of Job

For some seventy years now scholars have been investigating the hymns of the New Testament. You might well ask, What's a hymn? and, How do I detect one? Why haven't New Testament scholars told me about the existence and purpose of these hymns? These are important questions and deserve answers. The answers I offer will be somewhat long but will get us going on our musical journey down memory lanes where seven New Testament hymns sound forth their praise of God and the Lord Jesus Christ.

A. WHAT IS A NEW TESTAMENT HYMN?

Rather than try to define a hymn in the abstract, allow me to point us in the direction of some very familiar hymns in the canonical Gospels. In Luke's Gospel we find in 1:46-55 the hymn, which is usually called Mary's *Magnificat*. Almost immediately following that song of praise, we find Zachariah's *Benedictus* in Luke 1:68-79. And in Luke 2:14 we discover the angels' *Gloria*. Luke 2:29-32 gives voice to Simeon's *Nunc Dimittis*. I have purposely given these hymns the Latin titles by which they are known in various liturgical traditions that use the Divine Office. The *Benedictus* is sung at lauds or morning prayer. Mary's *Magnificat* finds a suitable place in vespers or evening prayer. The *Nunc Dimittis* fits very well into the last public prayer of the day, compline. The angels' Gloria serves as the base for the Gloria which is sung during Mass on festive days. Thus, the liturgical tradition has detected the hymnic nature of these songs of praise and has given them a prominent place in the church's daily praise of God.

In addition to the clues which the Church's liturgical tradition give us that Luke's four songs are hymns, we have those provided by contemporary English editions of the New Testament. (I will quote primarily from the New American Bible [NAB], and occasionally from the New Revised Standard Version [NRSV] where noted.) The editors of the NAB have set off the four Lukan passages from the rest of Luke 1–2, indicating that in their judgment these sections are not prose but poetic/hymnic. If you have a NAB available, please interrupt your reading to see if I'm right. If you have a NRSV, you will note that its editors have also indented the four hymnic passages from the rest of the text of Luke 1–2. Through the editorial policy of separating poetry from prose by some indentation, the editors are telling us that in their opinion these verses are not prose but poetry.

So now we have the precedent of the Church's liturgical tradition and the judgment of the editors of the NAB and NRSV that four passages in Luke 1–2 are hymns. Let's move from this external testimony to some internal evidence. Before getting specifically into that evidence, I would, however, advise my reader that the terms *poetry* and *hymn* have meant different things to different people over the centuries. For example, I recently compared the poetry of Shakespeare's *Antony and Cleopatra* to that of one of Emily Dickinson's crisp and short poems. Then I compared both of those works to a contemporary poem, *Shoelace,* by Roger Fanning (Glueck 1993, 69). In brief and as one would suspect, there were significant differences.

Although Markus Barth (1974, 7–8) gives eleven criteria and Ethelbert Stauffer (1955, 337–38) twelve for detecting the presence of hymnic material in the New Testament, the common consensus points to two general criteria. Because of his succinctness and clarity of expression I quote Peter T. O'Brien's description of these criteria: "Recent scholarship has drawn attention to two criteria for discerning hymnic material in the NT: (a) *stylistic:* a certain rhythmical lilt when the passages are read aloud, the presence of *parallelismus membrorum* (i.e., an arrangement into couplets), the semblance of some metre, and the presence of rhetorical devices such as alliteration, *chiasmus,* and antithesis; and (b) *linguistic:* an unusual vocabulary, particularly the presence of theological terms, which is different from the surrounding context" (1991, 188–89).

Lest these two criteria remain somewhat abstract, let me apply them to the Jewish-Christian hymn we treated ever so briefly above—Mary's *Magnificat* (Luke 1:46-55). I employ briefly the second criterion—that of linguistic difference from its context—with the simple remark that much of the vocabulary of Mary's hymn comes from the Old Testament, especially Hannah's song of praise in 1 Samuel 2:1-10. This "special vocabulary" separates it from its context. Let me spend more time with the first criterion, that of style, and give special attention to *parallelismus membrorum.* The literary form of New Testament hymns often follows the regular (Jewish) way of composing hymns, that is, they use parallelism of members/lines. These parallelisms may say the same thing in similar words (synonymous parallelism), may say the same thing in a complementary way (synthetic parallelism), or may further the thought by means of a contrast (antithetic parallelism).

As Joseph Fitzmyer has observed (1981, 360), Mary's *Magnificat* provides a splendid example of parallelism. The introduction to the hymn is found in vv. 46b–47 and is followed by two strophes: vv. 48–50 and 51–53. Vv. 54–55 form the conclusion of the hymn.

It should be also noted that v. 48 is often taken to be a Lukan composition.

Let me prepare your eyes to detect the parallelisms of Mary's hymn by stating that the lines of the introduction are set in synonymous parallelism, since soul/spirit and proclaims/rejoices mean about the same thing. Lines two and three of the first strophe are set in synthetic parallelism, for God's holiness is complemented by God's mercy. The lines of the second strophe are largely set in antithetic parallelism and manifest a theology of reversal of expectations. The conclusion displays synthetic parallelism. The trained eye might also detect two other stylistic features which enhance the pleasant flow of the hymn. First, the first strophe ends with mention of God's mercy; the conclusion also notes God's mercy. Second, the second strophe develops a *chiasmus*, in which the various elements form the Greek letter *chi* or a cross; the negatives *disperse, throw down,* and *send away empty* bracket the positives *lifted up* and *filled with good things*. Put in other terms, if *a* is negative and *b* is positive, we have the structure *a/a/b/b/a*.

Introduction
46b   My soul proclaims the greatness of the Lord;
47   my spirit rejoices in God my savior

First Strophe
48   For he has looked upon his handmaid's lowliness
      behold, from now on will all ages call be blessed
49   The Mighty One has done great things for me,
      and holy is his name
50   His mercy is from age to age
      to those who fear him

Second Strophe
51   He has shown might with his arm,
      dispersed the arrogant of mind and heart
52   He has thrown down the rulers from their thrones
      but lifted up the lowly
53   The hungry he has filled with good things,
      the rich he has sent away empty

Conclusion
54   He has helped Israel his servant,

remembering his mercy
55   According to his promise to our fathers,
       to Abraham and to his descendants forever (NAB).

Granting that there are hymns in the New Testament and that criteria exist by which we might detect their presence, how might we describe them? I follow the minimalist description of Stephen E. Fowl, who collapses the stylistic and linguistic criteria into the words *exalted* and *poetic:* ". . . these passages represent reflection on an exalted religious figure in language that could justifiably be called poetic" (1990, 16–17). Thus, hymns can be in honor of God or Lord Jesus, but also of Wisdom or the Word personified—all exalted figures. And the poetry of the hymn's composition may vary from parallelism of lines to contrasting strophes and may even tell a story rather than just sing out abstract praise, line after line, in honor of the exalted figure.

B. How Many New Testament Hymns Are There?

In his book on the hymn of Philippians 2:6-11, Ralph P. Martin, a master in the study of New Testament hymns, has this to say about the number of hymns in the New Testament (1993, 19):

> A number of putative hymns have been located, but no attempt has been made to place them in families. The following classification may, therefore, be suggested:
>
> (i)   the Lukan canticles
> (ii)   hymns in the Apocalypse
> (iii) Jewish-Christian fragments and ejaculations ('Amen, Hallelujah, Hosa'na, Marana tha, 'Abba)
> (iv)   distinctively Christian forms. The fourth section may be subdivided. But this classification is not rigid; and examples tend to overspill from one category into another. Any one hymn may be classified in more than one way:
> (a)   sacramental (Eph. v.14; Tit. iii.4-7); (with hesitation Rom. vi.1-11; Eph. ii.19-22)
> (b)   meditative (Eph. i.3-14; Rom. viii.31-9; I Cor. xiii)
> (c)   confessional (I Tim. vi.11-16; II Tim. ii.11-13)
> (d)   Christological (Heb. i.3; Col. i.15-20; I Tim. iii.16; John i.1-14; I Pet. i.18-21; ii.21-5; iii.18-21; Phil. ii.6-11)

It might be observed that four of the hymns which I treat pertain to Martin's category of Christological hymns (Col 1:15-20; 1 Tim 3:16; 1 Pet 3:18-21; Phil 2:6-11), one belongs to his category of sacramental hymns (Titus 3:4-7), another fits into his category of confessional hymns (2 Tim 2:11-13), and one (Eph 2:14-16) doesn't fit any of his categories. Now is not the time to expatiate on reasons for or against the hymnic nature of the passages Martin has listed. In subsequent chapters of this book I will have ample opportunity to give the reasons why I consider all the New Testament passages I have selected, even Ephesians 2:14-16, to be hymnic.

At the risk of overburdening my readers, I mention a scholarly refinement. Many scholars call hymns creeds and vice versa. This fluidity of terminology should not confuse us, because sometimes the content of a hymn is creedal. If I might, I bring our master teacher, Ralph Martin, back to the podium to share his wisdom with us: "It is not a simple business to separate the two types of early Christian literature. . . . We may say that the first confessions of faith tended to be expressed in short, simple sentences like 'Jesus is the Christ', or 'Jesus Christ is Lord', whereas the hymns represent a longer statement of the Person and work of Christ (as in Philippians 2,6-11; Colossians 1,15-20) . . ." (1974, 53). The interested reader might want to check the "Annotated Bibliography" of this chapter under the name of Ethelbert Stauffer, whose twelve criteria for ascertaining the presence of creedal formulae in the New Testament are similar to the eleven criteria which Markus Barth proposes for detecting the presence of New Testament hymns. Advanced students might want to pay special attention to my chapter on 1 Peter 3:18-22 where I consider how various hymnic, creedal, and catechectical traditions mutually interpret one another.

C. WHAT ARE THE SOURCES FOR THE NEW TESTAMENT HYMNS?

I remarked earlier that many scholars are of the opinion that the source for much of Mary's *Magnificat* (Luke 1:46-55) was the Old Testament, especially Hannah's song in 1 Samuel 2:1-10. At this introductory junction we might profitably raise a question: Is the Old Testament the only source for the style and content of

New Testament hymns? The answer is no. There are other models for New Testament hymns than those of the Old Testament, and the content for New Testament hymns arises from sources other than the Old Testament. What evidence do I give for my apodictic statements? Let me consider two examples from the vast body of Jewish hymns, psalms, and odes edited by James H. Charlesworth (1985, 607–771). One is from *Pseudo-Philo,* and the other one is prayer three from the "Hellenistic Synagogal Prayers." The style of each one is different; both are influenced by a type of wisdom tradition.

Daniel J. Harrington dates *Pseudo-Philo,* which has sixty-five chapters and is a rewriting of the Bible, to the time of Jesus. This work, originally written in Hebrew, is now only extant in Latin. It stems from Palestine and is "a witness to the understanding of the Bible in the Palestinian synagogues prior to C.E. 70 . . ." (1985, 302). I quote most of Hannah's prayer as found in chapter 51 of *Pseudo-Philo* (Harrington 1985, 365–66). We recall the story: God answered Hannah's prayers and delivered her from her humiliation of being childless. To Hannah and Elkanah, her husband, was born Samuel, a mighty judge and prophet and inaugurator of Israel's first king. Readers might want to compare *Pseudo-Philo*'s version of Hannah's prayer with that found in 1 Samuel 2:1-10, which is also the most comprehensive parallel for Mary's *Magnificat* in Luke 1:46-55.

While this hymn is different from both 1 Samuel 2:1-10 and Luke 1:46-55 because of its expansiveness, it cannot avoid the parallelisms so beloved by Jewish authors. I note two parallelisms. The first four lines of 51:3 are set in beautiful synonymous parallelism. "Voice," "speech," "mouth," and "lips" all say the same thing. Also, see the last two lines of 51:4 for a good example of antithetical parallelism, as "sterility" and "fecundity in childbearing" are contrasted.

I commence with verse two of chapter 51 wherein the priest Eli speaks to Hannah:

> 51:2 And Eli said to her, "You have not asked alone, but the people have prayed for this. This is not your request alone, but it was promised previously to the tribes. And through this boy your

womb has been justified so that you might provide advantage for the peoples and set up the milk of your breasts as a fountain for the twelve tribes."

51:3   And on hearing this, Hannah prayed and said,
"Come to my voice, all you nations,
and pay attention to my speech, all you kingdoms,
because my mouth has been opened that I should speak
and my lips have been commanded to sing a hymn to the Lord.
Drip, my breasts, and tell your testimonies,
because you have been commanded to give milk.
For he who is milked from you will be raised up,
and the people will be enlightened by his words,
and he will show to the nations the statutes,
and his horn will be exalted very high."

51:4   "And so I will speak my words openly,
because from me will arise the ordinance of the Lord,
and all men will find the truth.
Do not hurry to say great things
or to bring forth from your mouth lofty words,
but delight in glorifying [God].
For when the light from which wisdom is to be born will go forth,
not those who possess many things will be said to be rich,
nor those who have borne in abundance will be called mothers.
For the sterile one has been satisfied in childbearing,
but she who had many children has been emptied. . . ."

51:6   Speak, speak, Hannah, and do not be silent.
Sing a hymn, daughter of Batuel,
about the miracles that God has performed with you.
Who is Hannah that a prophet is born from her?
Or who is the daughter of Batuel that she should bear the light to
    the peoples?
Rise up, you also, Elkanah, and gird your loins.
Sing a hymn about the wonders of the Lord.
Because Asaph prophesied in the wilderness about your son, saying,
"Moses and Aaron were among his priests,
And Samuel was there among them."
Behold the word has been fulfilled,
and the prophecy has come to pass.
And these words will endure

until they give the horn to his anointed one
and power be present at the throne of his king.
And let my son stay here and serve
until he be made a light for this nation.

As I mentioned earlier, Hannah's hymn in *Pseudo-Philo* utilizes wisdom motifs. Cheryl Anne Brown correctly directs our attention to the graphic image of 51:2 ("the milk of her breasts is a fountain for the twelve tribes"). Here and in 51:4, line seven, the author uses the symbols associated with wisdom. See Sirach 15:2-3: "[Wisdom] will come to meet him like a mother. . . . She will feed him with the bread of learning, and give him the water of wisdom to drink" (NRSV). Further, see the wisdom reflection of the Jewish philosopher Philo of Alexandria, a contemporary of St. Paul, in his work *On Drunkenness* 31: "Accordingly wisdom is represented by some one of the beings of the divine company as speaking of herself in this manner: 'God created me as the first of his works, and before the beginning of time did he establish me.' For it was necessary that all the things which came under the head of the creation must be younger than the mother and nurse of the whole universe." Cheryl Anne Brown has rightly observed: "As a Wisdom figure, she (Hannah) offers the promise that Wisdom will indeed give birth to a new leader, who will provide the leadership the people have prayed and longed for, who will enlighten the nation—and even all people" (1992, 173).

In its expansiveness and in its fostering of wisdom imagery Hannah's hymn in *Pseudo-Philo* 51 is a good example of how Jewish prayers differed from one another and thus were not bound to the same style, vocabulary, and theology. We will see something similar in my second quotation, from a body of prayers which has been titled "Hellenistic Synagogal Prayers." While further studies about these prayers are necessary, the following points are clear. They consist of sixteen Jewish prayers which are found among books seven and eight of the fourth-century Christian work called the *Apostolic Constitutions*. These prayers often use the terminology of a hellenistic philosophy, similar to that found in the Book of Wisdom and in the works of Philo of Alexandria. Because of these terminological parallels I would date the "Hellenistic

Synagogal Prayers," which were originally composed in Greek, to
the first century C.E. I employ the translation of D. R. Darnell and
the editorial remarks of J. H. Charlesworth (1985, 671–97).

I quote from Prayer Three, but omit much of its recounting of
the creation of the heavens, water, and land. The observant reader
will immediately note how different this narrative prayer is, not
only in content but also in style, from that of Hannah in *Pseudo-
Philo* 51 and from that of Mary in Luke 1:46-55.

1   Blessed are you, O Lord, King of the ages,
       who through the Word made everything,
       and through him in the beginning ordered that which was
          unprepared;
2   who separated waters from waters with a firmament,
       and put a lively spirit in these;
3   who settled the earth (firmly),
       and stretched out heaven,
       and ordered the exact arrangement of each one of the creatures.
4   For by your conception, O Master, order has beamed with joy

         . . . .

15   Thereafter were prepared races of differing living creatures:
        those found on dry land,
        those living in water,
        those traversing the air,
        (and) amphibians.
16   And by the skilled Wisdom of your forethought
        is given to each one the appropriate providence.
17   For just as she was not exhausted in bringing forth differing
          races,
        neither has she neglected to make for each one a different
          providence.
18   And the goal of the creative work—
        the rational living creature, the world citizen—
19   having given order by your Wisdom, you created, saying,
        Let us make man according to our image and likeness;
20   having declared him a (micro)cosm of the cosmos,
        having formed for him the body out of the four elements;
21   and having prepared for him the soul out of non-being,
        and having given to him fivefold perception,
        and having placed over the perceptions a mind, the holder of
          the reins of the soul.

22   And in addition to all these things, O Master, Lord,
     who can worthily describe the movement of rain-producing
        clouds,
     the flashing forth of lightning, the clashing of thunders;
23   for the supplying of appropriate nourishment,
     and the blending of complex atmospheres?
24   But when man was disobedient,
     You took away his deserved life.
25   You did not make it disappear absolutely, but for a time,
26   having put (him) to sleep for a little (while),
     and by an oath you have called (him forth) to new birth.
27   You have loosed the boundary of death,
     You who are the Maker of life for the dead.

It is impossible in the confines of this book to provide an extensive commentary on this beautiful but involved prayer. A few
remarks will have to suffice. First, this hymnic prayer will help us
appreciate, more than Old Testament psalms, the type of philosophical background which certain hymn makers possessed. In
our discussions of Colossians 1:15-20 we will have occasion to
make further observations along this line. Second, while this
hymnic prayer may not employ the style of parallelism so dominant in Mary's *Magnificat* (Luke 1:46-55) and even present in
Hannah's prayer in *Pseudo-Philo,* it has its own stylistic niceties.
See, for example, the use of the passive participles at the beginning of lines nineteen through twenty-one: "having given," "having declared," "having formed," etc.

D. WHENCE THE PROFOUND CONTENT OF
THE NEW TESTAMENT HYMNS?

We have spent a considerable amount of space on the style of
different hymns and have only broached the subject of their content when we talked about the possible influence from the Old
Testament wisdom literature on Hannah's hymn in *Pseudo-Philo*
51 and Prayer Three of the "Hellenistic Synagogal Prayers." Now
is the time to respond to a query which is always raised: How did
the earliest Christians formulate such deeply theological hymns,
as the one found in Philippians 2:6-11, within twenty years after

Jesus' death? It seems to me that the answer to this question has two parts. One deals with profound Christology. The other focuses on the meteoric rise of this Christology.

D.1. THE RISE OF PROFOUND CHRISTOLOGY

The best, but perhaps not the most satisfying, answer to the question of the origins of the profound Christology of the New Testament hymns is the eschatological gift of the Holy Spirit in the earliest Christian communities. While the early chapters of the Acts of the Apostles may contain more theology than history, they point to the first century C.E. conviction that the Spirit of Pentecost inspired the worship and mission of the first Christian men and women.

Paul's First Letter to the Corinthians gives witness to his conviction and experience in the 50s of the first Christian century that the Holy Spirit was very active in Christian life and worship. See, for example, 1 Corinthians 14:1: "Pursue love, but strive eagerly for the spiritual gifts, above all that you may prophecy." See also 1 Corinthians 14:26: "So what is to be done, brothers and sisters? When you assemble, one has a psalm, another an instruction, a revelation, a tongue, or an interpretation. Everything should be done for building up." Among other gifts, Paul refers here to the Spirit's gift of psalm making; and here, I would suggest, we are on the brink of getting ourselves away from the true but speculative answer that the Holy Spirit was behind the profound Christology of the earliest Christians and putting ourselves into the hymn-makers' workshop.

Martin Hengel (1983, 78–96, 188–90), followed by Ralph P. Martin (1982, 37–49), has argued that the earliest creeds and hymns were messianic readings of Psalms 2; 8; 22; 110; 118. Without going into all the complexities, I note that the earliest Christians interpreted their experience of the risen and exalted Lord and the gift of his Spirit on the basis of Old Testament Psalms. Because of their Spirit-filled experience these Christians were able to interpret these psalms as referring to Jesus the Messiah. Using the NRSV, I sample New Testament use of one of these Messianic psalms. Psalm 110:1 reads: "The Lord says to my Lord, 'Sit at my right hand until I make your enemies your footstool.'" Hengel correctly detects reflection of Psalm 110:1 behind the creedal passage Ephesians 1:20-22: "God put this power to work in the Messiah when he raised him from the dead *and seated him at his right hand in the heavenly places. . . . And he has put all things under his feet*" (italics mine). Hengel is also right on target in highlighting how Psalm 110:1 is reflected in Romans 8:34: "Who is to condemn? It is Christ Jesus, who died, yes, who was raised, who *is at the right hand of God,* who indeed intercedes for us" (italics mine).

Hengel is not saying that full-blown hymns are present in either Ephesians 1:20-22 or Romans 8:34. Rather we have evidence of the earliest Christians' utilization of psalms to give voice to their experience of the exalted Messiah Jesus. When we treat in detail the hymn in 1 Peter 3:18-22, we will see how the messianic Psalm 110 influenced the formulation and Christology of this hymn.

But how do we get from creedal one-liners that profess Messiah Jesus to be at the right hand of God, to full-blown Christologically profound hymns like Philippians 2:6-11 by the year 50 C.E.? Surely, the Holy Spirit is involved. But I would also venture to include two human factors in this Christological enterprise. First, the short messianic hymns/creeds were expanded narratively. For example, the hymn in Philippians 2:6-11 puts Messiah Jesus' exaltation at the end of the story of his taking the form of a slave, becoming human, and enduring a humiliating death on a cross. At this stage we must remember that the narratives which we call Gospels did not exist. One could make a case that the first narratives of Jesus' meaning for the universe were formulated in some of the New Testament hymns.

The second factor was the use of wisdom theology as found, for example, in Proverbs 8, Sirach 24, and Wisdom 2–5. I am going to quote some salient verses from Proverbs 8, but first allow me to predetermine your reading of these verses. Imagine yourself back in the first century C.E. You know of Jesus' life, his awful death by crucifixion, and his resurrection and exaltation to God's right hand. You know that you have received of Jesus' Spirit and participate in a Spirit-animated church. And now you are wondering about Jesus' relationship—before his birth, before time began—to God. And you chance upon and read Proverbs 8:22-31:

"The Lord created me at the beginning of his work, the first of his acts of long ago. Ages ago I was set up, at the first, before the beginning of the earth. . . . When he established the heavens, I was there. . . . When he marked out the foundations of the earth, then I was beside him, like a master worker; and I was daily his delight, rejoicing before him always, rejoicing in his inhabited world and delighting in the human race" (NRSV).

In our discussion of individual hymns we will have occasion to return to the paramount role which wisdom theology played in the development and formulation of New Testament hymns which sing of Christ's preexistence. In my final chapter I will return to this point and broaden it. In relating my conclusion to my introduction, I am creating an *inclusio,* a rhetorical feature beloved by biblical writers. Further, since my conclusion will expand on what I have written here, I will also be fashioning a type of synthetic parallelism. In any case, here I just want to whet your appetite.

In conclusion, I mention that Martin Hengel (1976, 2) is of the opinion that between 30–50 C.E. there was more Christological development than between 50–700 C.E. And remember that the years 50–700 C.E. would include the Councils of Nicaea and Chalcedon, which defined who Jesus was and is. As Hengel says in another place: "To put it briefly, the hymn to Christ served as a living medium for the progressive development of christological thinking. It begins with the messianic psalms and ends in the prologue to John" (1983, 95).

D.2. WHY THE VERY RAPID RISE OF PROFOUND CHRISTOLOGY?

It seems that the more questions we answer, the more questions we generate. If the earliest Christians composed profound Christological hymns within a thirty-year period, 30–60 C.E., how did they do it? How can we visualize what was going on behind the scenes during these thirty years? If we grant that the wisdom traditions supplied much of the thought for the Christology of the New Testament hymns, I offer the following scholarly observations to aid our visualization.

First, we must take into consideration that the first Christians, who generally were neither nobles nor wealthy, included many skilled and educated people who might be slaves or freedmen.

Granting all the differences between Jewish, Greek, and Latin cultures, I borrow data from Sandra R. Joshel and apply them to the New Testament situation, in which Rome ruled the roost. Through her study of first and second century C.E. Roman commemorative inscriptions from slaves, freed slaves, and unprivileged freeborn citizens who identified themselves by their occupations, Joshel has made a list of "Occupational Titles in Roman Inscriptions" (1992, 176–82). Seven of these titles are important for our consideration, and all are in Latin: (1) *cantor-trix*, singer, (2) *citharoedus*, lyre player and singer, (3) *hymnologus*, singer of hymns, (4) *musicus*, musician, (5) *philosophos*, philosopher, (6) *poeta*, poet, and (7) *symphoniacus*, musician.

The musicians, etc., were often slaves in upper-class urban households, which had need of tens, sometimes hundreds, of slaves, who were often buried in the burial vault *(columbarium)* set aside for the *familia* of the master. One such person is *Scirtus symphoniacus Cornelianus* who belonged to the *familia* of the Statilii (Joshel 1992, 41). Scirtus finds his identity as a musician *(symphoniacus)* at Cornelia's service. I surmise from this information that the slaves who came to worship, e.g., in the Christian house church in Philippi, which was a Roman colony, may well have been poets, philosophers, and highly trained musicians from that household or the wealthy household next door or down the street a mile or so away. Now they no longer only served their master and mistress, but may also have provided poems and hymns and songs—with accompaniment of kithara and/or lyre—for their brothers and sisters in the Lord Jesus.

To help us further in our visualization, I note that the inscription of one of the freedmen studied by Joshel mentions that he had a shop. So the hymn maker from Caelimontano (Joshel 1992, 206, n. 30) went to work daily and made his living through his ability to compose and sing hymns. In modern terms, we would say that he spent weekdays composing and on weekends he hauled his kithara and lyre to various locations to make music for those who had contracted for his services.

Speaking of kithara and lyre, let me enhance our visualization more by stating that there is sufficient evidence from the studies of Johannes Quasten (1983, 72–73, 121–22) that the kithara and lyre were used during earliest Christian worship in the Pauline churches. Moreover, Quasten (1983, 137–39) has reminded us that freeborn boys and girls received training in music from their earliest years. I add that it would seem valid to infer that slaves whose musical gifts were detected early would have also been trained for the service of their master or mistress or for possible resale value. Some of these slaves became the hymn writers and musicians found on the inscriptions studied by Joshel. Finally, Quasten firmly makes a point about the inclusive nature of the earliest singing of hymns: "Women commonly and universally took part in liturgical singing in earliest Christian times on account of the notion of the spiritual koinonia, which expressed itself in community singing" (1983, 85). In brief, a musical culture existed at the time the New Testament hymns were composed and performed.

To ground my points more firmly in first century C.E. sources, I consider Philo of Alexandria, who describes religious musical composition which paralleled the making of New Testament hymns. In his work *On the Contemplative Life,* Philo describes the *therapeutae,* men and women who had abandoned the world for the sake of solitude and contemplation. On the seventh day of the week they gathered together, women in one area and men in another, to worship God, break bread, celebrate their common vocation. About their music Philo writes: "Then they sing hymns which have been composed in honor of God in many meters and tunes, at one time all singing together, and at another moving their hands and dancing in corresponding harmony, and uttering in an inspired manner songs of thanksgiving, and at another time regular odes, and performing all necessary strophes and antistrophes" (Yonge 1993, 706). Philo notes that this sober, religious merrymaking went on all night long. If the earliest Christian communities were anything like the *therapeutae,* then it is small wonder that they composed their own hymns and enjoyed singing them during worship on their own seventh day.

How could the first Christians compose these hymns so soon after Jesus' death? Let me use an in-house Franciscan example to fashion an illustrative answer to this question, borrowing heavily from the work of my confrere, Fr. Robert M. Hutmacher, O.F.M., who is a composer of hymns. His recent research deals with thirteenth-century hymns in honor of St. Clare of Assisi (1993, no.

51). In 1257, a mere four years after St. Clare's death, a hymn was created in honor of this exalted person. This six-stanza Latin hymn is resplendent with a play on the word Clare, which can mean *light, clear, flame,* and *bright.* The hymn also is radiant with rhyme. Already from this hymn's Latin title we catch a glimpse of its beauty and playfulness. The title, "O Clara, Luce Clarior," might be translated "O Clare, More Clear and Radiant Than the Light."

In an effort to give a clearer indication of the play of words and the rhyme in the Latin of "O Clara, Luce Clarior," I give my own English rendition of its first, fifth, and last stanzas:

> O Clare, brighter than the light,
> Daughter of the eternal light
> This day is made more solemn
> Through our celebration of your solemnity.
>
> Now in the realm of the lights,
> The daughter co-reigning with the Father,
> Give to the masses who thee follow
> Righteous paths to follow.
>
> To the Father, First Born, and Flame of Light
> All praise, honor, and glory.
> May the prayers of St. Clare
> Commend us to the Light.

At the risk of repeating what I have said earlier, allow me briefly to make two points of comparison between this thirteenth-century hymn and the first-century New Testament hymns. We moderns generally, because of our technological advancements, are prejudiced and think that the ancients were far inferior to us in knowledge and abilities. The hymn maker(s) who composed "O Clara, Luce Clarior," lived more than 725 years ago and on most accounts did rather well in composing this great hymn, using the hymn-making tools available to them. Their accomplishment suggests that people during Jesus' and Paul's lifetime—nineteen hundred years ago—might also have been able to compose some excellent hymns. Second, the timing of the composition of "O Clara, Luce Clarior" shows that a masterpiece could be composed shortly after an exalted figure had died.

E. THE ROLE OF NEW TESTAMENT HYMNS IN THE SOCIALIZATION OF MEN AND WOMEN INTO CHRISTIAN FAITH AND LIFESTYLE

I cannot conclude this Introduction without piggybacking on some relevant recent studies on New Testament ethics. Stephen E. Fowl (1990) and Wayne A. Meeks (1993) make many valid points in their explorations of the ways in which New Testament narratives, lists of virtues, creeds, and hymns have shaped and formed Christian consciousness and conscience. Allow me to use some homely examples on how New Testament hymns might have functioned in their time. In my chapter on Philippians 2:6-11 I will provide scholarly details on how that hymn was used to shape the conscience of the Philippians.

I think of the aha experience I had recently as I was listening to a compact disc, "Fennell Conducts Porter & Gershwin." The vast majority of the twenty-four songs on this CD were known to me, yet I didn't remember having ever listened to them. They were part of my socialization as I grew up and were probably conveyed over radio, in school, at the movies—one might say in the air I breathed. I've had a similar experience when listening to the twenty-three songs on the CD, "Frederick Fennell Conducts the Music of Leroy Anderson," e.g., the delightful works "Sleigh Ride" and "The Syncopated Clock." Or I think of the socialization process involved in growing up a Roman Catholic in the "old days," when Latin was used. Almost all Catholics my age could sing the Latin *Missa De Angelis* in Gregorian chant for Mass. Also, for us in religious orders there were the Marian hymns we learned in Latin. How well these hymns nurtured reverence and devotion, perhaps more so than many a catechism lesson.

Of course, these examples date me and tell all and sundry from what social class I came, and this is inevitable. For whether my skin is wrinkled or smooth, white or brown, I cannot wiggle out of it. Those younger than I will have to search out their own positive examples of American or other songs which socialized them into American society and at the same time helped shape their value system. Or my readers may understand my point by reflecting upon the fact that music can socialize people negatively.

Recently parents have joined together to force authorities to ban certain socially toxic lyrics from contemporary songs, for they don't want their children socialized by such harmful music.

Might our positive experience of being socialized into civil and religious cultures through music suggest that New Testament hymns functioned in the same way for the earliest Christians? Surely, I have no tape-recorded proof. But it doesn't take much scholarly imagination to visualize Christians leaving an agape meal during which, as Pliny reports (110 C.E.), they ssng a hymn to Christ as God, and hummed its music as they went their way. These Christians would also find the tune of such hymns recurring in their minds and on their lips daily as they went about their business, and in this way their faith was strengthened against the powers of fate and evil as they sang that every knee must bend at Jesus' name (Phil 2:10).

F. Conclusion

During this chapter we have initiated our musical journey down the memory lanes of our New Testament hymns. To enliven our journey, we have played a game of question and answer. Hopefully, during the course of our game I have answered many of your questions and have sparked others in your mind. You might find it very helpful to return to this introductory chapter from time to time as you work through the remaining chapters which focus on individual New Testament hymns. This chapter is foundational and will be presupposed in what follows.

A final word: as you read through this book and nibble on its insights, joyfully take to heart these words penned some nineteen-hundred years ago: "Let the word of Christ dwell in you richly, as in all wisdom you teach and admonish one another, singing psalms, hymns, and spiritual songs with gratitude in your hearts to God" (Col 3:16, NAB; see Eph 5:19).

Annotated Bibliography

Barth, Markus. *Ephesians 1–3*. Anchor Bible 34A. Garden City: Doubleday, 1974. Barth's eleven criteria for ascertaining the presence

of New Testament hymns are very similar to the two general crite-
ria enumerated by Stephen E. Fowl. In my chapter on Titus 3:4-7,
I detail what Barth's eleven criteria are as I utilize them to show why
I am of the opinion that Titus 3:4-7 is a hymn.

Brown, Cheryl Anne. *No Longer Be Silent: First Century Jewish Portraits
of Biblical Women.* Louisville: Westminster/John Knox, 1992. Brown
studies how Pseudo-Philo and Josephus describe the same biblical
women. Pseudo-Philo's *Biblical Antiquities* reveals "a community in
which women knew and taught scripture; communicated freely
God's messages of comfort, hope, reproof, and exhortation; led in
worship and the singing of hymns; and interceded before God for
the community" (218).

Charlesworth, James H., ed. *The Old Testament Pseudepigrapha.* Vol. 2.
Garden City: Doubleday, 1985. There is considerable material in
"Prayers, Psalms, and Odes," 607–771. I would also recommend
Charlesworth's article, "Jewish Hymns, Odes, and Prayers (ca. 167
B.C.E.–35 C.E.)," in *Early Judaism and its Modern Interpreters.* Eds.
Robert A. Kraft and George W. E. Nickelsburg, 411–36. Philadel-
phia/Atlanta: Fortress/Scholars, 1986. Most of this hymnic mate-
rial, according to Charlesworth, needs extensive study and must be
liberated from the assumptions that Judaism had a monolithic
sameness and that all Jewish prayer forms were fixed at the time of
Jesus. Further, Charlesworth is correct to insist that the study of
Jewish prayer forms are of paramount importance for the proper
study of the New Testament.

Charlesworth, James H., ed., and D. R. Darnell, trans. "Hellenistic
Synagogal Prayers (Second to Third Century A.D.)." *The Old
Testament Pseudepigrapha.* Vol. 2, 671–97. Garden City: Double-
day, 1985.

Fitzmyer, Joseph A. *The Gospel According to Luke (I–IX): Introduction,
Translation, and Notes.* Anchor Bible 28A. Garden City: Doubleday,
1981. An excellent commentary on all aspects of Luke's Gospel.

Fowl, Stephen E. *The Story of Christ in the Ethics of Paul: An Analysis of the
Function of the Hymnic Material in the Pauline Corpus.* Journal for the
Study of the New Testament Supplement Series 36. Sheffield: JSOT
Press, 1990. A helpful study with individual chapters on the hymns
of Philippians 2:6-11; Colossians 1:15-20; and 1 Timothy 3:16.

Glueck, Louise, ed. *The Best American Poetry 1993.* New York:
Macmillan, 1993.

Harrington, D. J. "Pseudo-Philo (First Century A.D.): A New Translation
and Introduction." *The Old Testament Pseudepigrapha.* Vol. 2. Ed.

James H. Charlesworth. Garden City: Doubleday, 1985. Harrington's complete treatment of *Pseudo-Philo* is on pp. 297–377.

Hengel, Martin. *The Son of God: The Origin of Christology and the History of Jewish-Hellenistic Religion.* Philadelphia: Fortress, 1976. A general work on the background of New Testament Christology.

Hengel, Martin. "Hymns and Christology." *Between Jesus and Paul: Studies in the Earliest History of Christianity,* 78–96, 188–90. Philadelphia: Fortress, 1983. This is a foundational article for any study of New Testament hymns.

Hutmacher, Robert M. *Clare and Francis: O Let the Faithful People Sing.* St. Bonaventure, N.Y.: Franciscan Institute Publications, 1993.

Joshel, Sandra R. *Work, Identity, and Legal Status at Rome: A Study of the Occupational Inscriptions.* Oklahoma Series in Classical Culture. Norman: University of Oklahoma Press, 1992. A vast amount of valuable data for New Testament scholars.

Martin, Ralph P. *Worship in the Early Church.* Rev. ed. Grand Rapids: Eerdmans, 1974. A basic, popular study on all aspects of worship.

Martin, Ralph P. "Some Reflections on New Testament Hymns." *Christ the Lord: Studies in Christology Presented to Donald Guthrie.* Ed. Harold H. Rowdon, 37–49. Leicester: Inter-Varsity, 1982. Martin continues to reflect on a theme which has occupied much of his scholarly life since his dissertation on the hymn of Philippians 2:6-11.

Martin, Ralph P. *Carmen Christi: Philippians ii.5-11 in Recent Interpretation and in the Setting of Early Christian Worship.* Rev. ed. with new preface. Grand Rapids: Eerdmans, 1983. The original was published in 1967.

Meeks, Wayne A. *The Origins of Christian Morality: The First Two Centuries.* New Haven: Yale University Press, 1993. A creative approach to the thorny question of the ethics of the New Testament.

O'Brien, Peter T. *The Epistle to the Philippians. A Commentary on the Greek Text.* New International Greek Testament Commentary Series. Grand Rapids: Eerdmans, 1991. An excellent commentary, whose influence on my studies will be noted in my chapter on the hymn of Philippians 2:6-11.

Quasten, Johannes. *Music & Worship in Pagan & Christian Antiquity.* Translated from rev. ed. of 1973; Washington: National Association of Pastoral Musicians, 1983. Quasten, generally known as a Patristics scholar, was a man of great learning.

Stauffer, Ethelbert. *New Testament Theology.* London: SCM, 1955. Although Stauffer's twelve criteria occur in his Appendix III as "Twelve Criteria of Creedal Formulae in the New Testament," they are similar to Markus Barth's eleven criteria for discovering the presence of a hymn in the New Testament.

Wilder, Amos N. *Theopoetic.* Philadelphia: Fortress, 1976. Wilder was a pioneer in the application of the insights of literary criticism to the New Testament.

Yonge, C. D., trans. *The Works of Philo: Complete and Unabridged.* New updated ed. Peabody: Henrickson, 1993. A clear and handy translation of Philo's considerable writings which provide many helpful parallels for interpreting New Testament thought and praxis.

III. CHAPTER 2

Let's Do a Background Check

As we delve into the New Testament hymns, we will notice that many of them are unfamiliar and perhaps not obvious. Take, for example, 1 Timothy 3:16:

> . . . Who was manifested in the flesh,
> vindicated in the spirit,
> seen by angels,
> proclaimed to the Gentiles,
> believed in throughout the world,
> taken up in glory (NAB).

In order to interpret a phrase like "seen by angels," we will have to do a background check. What background, as understood through sources contemporaneous with the New Testament, enables us to interpret such phrases most satisfactorily? In what follows I will provide some elementary guidance about the tools employed by those who specialize in checking New Testament backgrounds.

A. BACKGROUND IN GENERAL

Let me use some illustrations to get us thinking about the significance of background. First, getting to know more and more about a person's background can be fundamental to striking up a deep and lasting friendship with that individual. Second, it sometimes happens that because friends and spouses have shared the same life over decades, they can conjure up profound memories by the mere mention of an event or the opening words of a song. A person who does not share their background is virtually ignorant of what the friends or spouses are talking about or to what they are referring. Class reunions thrive on the shared background and memories of the "good old days."

On an academic level, it seems to me that history becomes fun when one detects the historical background of a seemingly strange practice. For example, I once wondered why ecclesiastical art depicts the lay woman St. Clare of Assisi (1197–1253) with a monstrance in her hand? Aren't only deacons and priests—i.e., men—allowed to touch the monstrance? On my search for an answer I discovered a book by Caroline Walker Bynum who writes this of St. Clare and her food-centered spirituality: "She shed tears before the holy food of the eucharist and approached it with awe. She once put an enemy to flight with the host. Her iconographic motif is the monstrance. She is thus associated visually as well as in written evidence with the emerging cult of the consecrated host. Furthermore, serving—especially feeding—others is a major theme in Clare's *vita*" (1987, 101). Through the good background which she provided on thirteenth-century practices and Clare's life, Bynum implicitly cautioned me that modern ecclesiastical legislation about who can or cannot touch the monstrance is irrelevant in interpreting a practice of earlier centuries. Finally, I should not be asking a canonical question about a metaphor—food—which is beyond canons and touches the very substance of our lives. Having seen the importance of background checks in general, let's shake hands with some possible backgrounds for New Testament hymns.

B. Backgrounds to New Testament Hymns

As I treat individual hymns I will explore in some detail the backgrounds I have selected to interpret the hymn. Here I want to provide some general comments about New Testament backgrounds. It is not my intention to discuss all possible New Testament backgrounds. Thus, for example, I will not deal with the Qumran literature.

The Old Testament will provide considerable background for many of the hymns, for it is commonly presupposed that their composers most likely sought in the Old Testament analogies for God's action in Jesus the Christ. See, for example, the fourth suffering servant psalm of Isaiah 52:13–53:12, especially 53:12 ("because he surrendered himself to death"), as possible background for interpreting Philippians 2:8 ("he humbled himself, becoming obedient to death"), of the hymn in Philippians 2:6-11. Another example is found in the way that Wisdom 7:25-27 might provide background for the hymn in Colossians 1:15-20. "For she [Wisdom] is an aura of the might of God and a pure effusion of the glory of the Almighty. . . . For she is the refulgence of the eternal light, the spotless mirror of the power of God, the image of his goodness. And she, who is one, can do all things, and renews everything while herself perduring."

And despite some skepticism in certain quarters, *the gnostic literature from Nag Hammadi* will at times manifest illuminating background for some New Testament hymns. In our consideration of 1 Timothy 3:16 I will indicate how the Nag Hammadi document *Apocryphon of John* may help us interpret the phrase "seen by angels." A host of methodological concerns swirl around the use of the chronologically later Nag Hammadi documents for interpreting the earlier New Testament documents. It is not my contention that some composers of New Testament hymns borrowed from later documents. Rather, I maintain that both may have drawn upon an earlier common pattern. I direct readers who are interested in more detail to the very insightful book by Pheme Perkins (1993). I have found particularly useful Perkins' notion of *mythemes* or "individual narrative units that are combined to make up each variant of a myth" (1993, 236). Thus, the entire myth, which might be dated two centuries later, need not be present before one determines the presence of a Gnostic theme in a New Testament hymn. Interested readers will find helpful material in the conclusion of this book where I address the role of myth as a means of universalizing meaning.

In chapter one I quoted from *The Old Testament Pseudepigrapha* (1983, 1985) edited by James H. Charlesworth. In the two volumes of this work scholars have provided apt introductions to and fresh translations of numerous noncanonical documents which date before, during, or just after New Testament times. In my chapter on the hymn in 1 Peter 3:18-22 I will employ First and Second Enoch as interpretive background for the puzzling statement: "In it he (Christ) also went to preach to the spirits in prison, who had once been disobedient" (1 Pet 3:19-20).

From time to time you might notice that commentators interpret one New Testament hymn on the basis of its similarity with *other New Testament hymns.* This way of interpreting a New Testament hymn can be quite insightful, but has some drawbacks. First, one may be interpreting the obscure by the equally obscure. Second, the interpreter may get trapped in a vicious circle. That is, I prove that X should be interpreted as I have interpreted Y. Yet my basis for interpreting Y the way I did was its similarity to X. To be more specific, interpreters often explain the first two lines of 1 Timothy 3:16 by reference to Romans 1:3-4 and 1 Peter 3:18:

Who was manifested in the flesh, vindicated in the spirit (1 Tim 3:16)	about his Son, descended from David according to the flesh . . . according to the spirit (Rom 1:3-4)	Put to death in the flesh, he was brought to life in the spirit (1 Pet 3:18).

While the parallels between 1 Timothy 3:16, Romans 1:3-4, and 1 Peter 3:18 are strong, especially with regard to the contrast of *flesh* and *spirit,* there are considerable differences, e.g., the use of the title "Son of God" for Jesus in Romans 1:3-4. I personally do not use the interpretive parallels of Romans 1:3-4 and 1 Peter 3:18 in my chapter on 1 Timothy 3:16.

Another key interpretive background is *contextualization.* For example, the meaning of a hymn can be determined from the way the author of a New Testament book utilized it in a new context. For example, in our discussion of 1 Timothy 3:16 I will show why the author of the Pastoral Epistles inserted this hymn, which celebrates Christ's manifestation "in the flesh," into an epistle wherein he is combating, in Paul's name, those who denied the goodness of God's creation. Each chapter of my book devotes a special section to the immediate and broader contexts of the particular hymn being discussed.

Another important background is the New Testament *itself.* Here I do not refer to the background material to be found in other New Testament hymns. Nor do I refer to the ways in which an author of a book in the New Testament has utilized the traditional hymn in a new context. Rather I refer to the way in which other New Testament writings may illuminate various lines in a hymn. For example, in my discussion of the hymn of 2 Timothy 2:11-13, I—along with other scholars—find helpful interpretive parallels of certain elements of that hymn in Paul's Letter to the Romans. That is, "If we have died with him, we shall also live with him" in 2 Timothy 2:11 is almost identical with Romans 6:8: "If, then we have died with Christ, we believe that we shall also live with him." Put another way, the author of the Pastoral Epistles may well have quoted hymns, some of whose lines were formulated in the Pauline idiom known from other Pauline epistles.

Although describing a period of time somewhat later than the New Testament, E. R. Dodds still accurately describes another major background for interpreting the New Testament hymns. These hymns were composed in *"an age of anxiety"* (1965). According to Dodds (and other scholars) everyone, whether Gentile, Jewish, Christian, or Gnostic, believed in the existence of malevolent angelic powers. Further, the belief was rampant that one's entire life was determined by fate. Perhaps, considering this background, it is small wonder that five of the seven hymns I feature in my book—1 Timothy 3:16, Philippians 2:6-11, Colossians 1:15-20, Ephesians 2:14-16, and 1 Peter 3:18-22—take pains to demonstrate how Jesus reigns above the angels or has vanquished the evil angels.

The many philosophical-theological works of the Hellenistic Jew *Philo of Alexandria,* a contemporary of Jesus and Paul, are filled with useful interpretive materials for our study of New Testament hymns. For example, in interpreting the meaning of the verb, "making peace," in Colossians 1:20, I happily draw upon a parallel in Philo.

Besides Judaism and Christianity there were *other religious movements* in the first century C.E. In my chapter on Titus 3:4-7 I find an illuminating example of the religious meaning of "rebirth" in the Hermetic Corpus. And in my Conclusion I call upon

Cleanthes' "Hymn to Zeus" and Lucius' "Aretalogy to Isis" to shed light on the longings of Hellenistic men and women for universal salvation.

Finally, Reinhard Deichgräber (1967) has exhorted us that we should never forget that the ultimate interpretive background is *the praise and worship of God.* There seems to be almost universal scholarly consensus that the New Testament hymns were used in worship and thus were meant to praise God. Scholars may argue vigorously with one another about whether Colossians 1:15-20 is best interpreted from a Wisdom or a Gnostic background. Yet they miss the boat of solid interpretation if they end up patting themselves on the back for having won an argument. Rather they should join their voices to those who praise Jesus "who is the image of the invisible God, the firstborn of all creation" (Col 1:15).

C. A NOTE ON *THE* NEW TESTAMENT CHRISTOLOGICAL HYMNS

Sometimes scholars give the impression that there is a fixed number of New Testament hymns by referring to *the* New Testament Christological hymns. It is the contention of this book that there is no closed canon or repertoire of New Testament hymns and also that there is no one single dominant interpretive background for these hymns. I will give some substance to my contentions by offering a brief review of two influential works on the subject.

In his monograph, Jack T. Sanders (1971) treats three hymns at considerable length: the prologue of John's Gospel (1:1-5, 9-11), Philippians 2:6-11, and Colossians 1:15-20. He gives less attention to what he terms "the shorter passages": Ephesians 2:14-16, Hebrews 1:3, 1 Timothy 3:16, and 1 Peter 3:18-22. His conclusion about the "historical religious background" of these hymns was: "Thus, rather than arguing that the redeemer motifs of the Odes of Solomon and of the Nag Hammadi texts stem from the New Testament, it would seem more appropriate to conclude that the three groups—New Testament Christological hymns, Nag Hammadi texts (especially the Apocalypse of Adam), and the Odes of Solomon—represent a more or less parallel development of concepts infiltrating the various religions of the eastern Mediterranean world around the beginning of the Christian era" (1971, 132).

In formulating his theory about the "historical religious background" of the New Testament hymns, Sanders gives important consideration to Israel's wisdom tradition, which, as we will see, is the exclusive background for these hymns according to Ben Witherington III. Sanders writes: "Thus it may be suggested that the New Testament Christological hymns had their formal matrix within the Wisdom school, and this of course coincides with the thesis that they represent a stage of a developing myth which had its prior development in Wisdom speculation" (1971, 136). Three pages later he comments: "The Wisdom circles of Judaism, then, where the thanksgiving hymn was most at home, seem to have provided the most convenient point of entry for redeemer motifs from other religions into Judaism, or to have provided the best possibility of a merger" (1971, 139). For an update, with no substantial change of position, on the historical religious background Sanders assigns to the New Testament Christological hymns, one can consult Sanders' recent article (1990).

I have some quibbles with Sanders' judgment about the background of the New Testament hymns he treats, for he presupposes "a developing myth" without stating the forces behind its development in one arena and not another. Further, he lacks sufficient evidence for his assertion that all New Testament Christological hymns belong to the literary genre of a "thanksgiving hymn" and are the "because" section of such a hymn, as they supply the reasons why the author and community give thanks (Sanders 1971, 1–5, 143). Moreover, I question his selection of "longer" and "shorter" hymns by asking who has determined that these hymns and no others make up *the* New Testament Christological hymns. In writing this book, I have culled the scholarly literature to ascertain whether scholars have found other Christological hymns in the New Testament. And they have. Based on this newer research, I have expanded the number of hymns I treat. And in my treatment of an enlarged repertoire of New Testament hymns it will become clear that Sanders' background does not apply to all of them; for example, 2 Timothy 2:11-13.

In his book, Ben Witherington III devotes a chapter to New Testament hymns (1994, 249–94) and describes his thesis as follows: "It is the major thesis of this chapter that the Christological hymn fragments found in the Pauline corpus, the Fourth Gospel, and Hebrews are fundamentally expressions of a Wisdom Christology that goes back to early Jewish Christianity and reflects the fact that some of the earliest Christological thinking about Jesus amounted to what today would be called a very 'high' Christology indeed" (1994, 249).

In his chapter on New Testament hymns Witherington discusses Philippians 2:6-11, Colossians 1:15-20, 1 Timothy 3:16, Hebrews 1:2-4, and John 1:1-5, 9-14. His major thesis falters because, according to his own admission, 1 Timothy 3:16 does not express a wisdom Christology: "Finally, this hymn is the *only one* amongst the generally recognized Christ hymns that does not strongly manifest a sapiential character, drawing on material especially from Sirach and the Wisdom of Solomon" (1994, 275). But neither does 1 Peter 3:18-22 manifest a sapiential character, as Witherington concedes (1994, 275). And it should be noted that Witherington dismisses, in one paragraph, the arguments that Ephesians 2:13-18 is a hymn, maintaining that "Eph. 2:13-18 is likely not a hymn but rather a theological reflection on the Colossians hymn" (1994, 272). Does Witherington omit Ephesians 2:13-18 from his list because it seems difficult to argue that there is a sapiential background behind it? In summary, if Witherington had included 1 Peter 3:18-22 and Ephesians 2:13-18 in his list of generally recognized Christ hymns, he would have found that not just one but three of his New Testament Christological hymns do not have a sapiential background. In other words, his thesis would be considerably weakened.

In conclusion, I would strongly suggest that the repertoire of New Testament Christological hymns has not been fixed, at least in the sense that Witherington means. Many of the passages which Sanders and Witherington have studied were first argued to be hymns in the early decades of the twentieth century. As the decades have rolled by, further research has pointed to the presence of additional Christological hymns in New Testament books. I would also humbly submit that no one background is able to explain all the New Testament Christological hymns. A multidimensional approach like the one I sketched earlier in this chapter and plan to use in my investigation of individual hymns may be more helpful and accurate. At the same time that I argue for a more comprehensive approach to the New Testament hymns than that provided by Sanders and Witherington, I do want to join my voice to theirs as we sing the refrain that the Wisdom tradition is a very important source for many significant New Testament hymns.

ANNOTATED BIBLIOGRAPHY

Bynum, Caroline Walker. *Holy Feast and Holy Fast: The Religious Significance of Food to Medieval Women.* Berkeley: University of California Press, 1987.

Charlesworth, James H., ed. *The Old Testament Pseudepigrapha.* Vols. 1 and 2. Garden City: Doubleday, 1983, 1985.

Deichgräber, Reinhard. *Gotteshymnus und Christushymnus in der frühen Christenheit: Untersuchungen zu Form, Sprache und Stil der frühchristlichen Hymnen.* Studien zur Umwelt des Neuen Testaments 5. Göttingen: Vandenhoeck and Ruprecht, 1967.

Dodds, E. R. *Pagan and Christian in an Age of Anxiety: Some Aspects of Religious Experience from Marcus Aurelius to Constantine.* Cambridge: Cambridge University Press, 1965.

Perkins, Pheme. *Gnosticism and the New Testament.* Minneapolis: Fortress, 1993. See especially pp. 93–108 ("Redeemer Myths and New Testament Hymns").

Sanders, Jack T. *The New Testament Christological Hymns: Their Historical Religious Background.* Society of New Testament Studies Monograph Series 15. Cambridge: Cambridge University Press, 1971. For a telling critique of Sanders' hypothesis of a "developing myth" and of the eight elements he assigns to this myth, see Elisabeth Schüssler Fiorenza, "Wisdom Mythology and the Christological Hymns of the New Testament." *Aspects of Wisdom in Judaism and Early Christianity.* Ed. Robert L. Wilken, 17–41, especially 22–26. Notre Dame: University of Notre Dame Press, 1975.

Sanders, Jack T. "Nag Hammadi, Odes of Solomon, and NT Christological Hymns." *Gnosticism & The Early Christian World: In Honor of James M. Robinson.* Forum Fascicles 2. Eds. James E. Goehring, Charles W. Hedrick, and Jack Sanders with Hans Dieter Betz, 51–66. Sonoma: Polebridge, 1990. On p. 59, no. 28, Sanders attempts to respond to Schüssler Fiorenza's criticism of his monograph. See previous entry.

Witherington III, Ben. *Jesus the Sage: The Pilgrimage of Wisdom.* Minneapolis: Fortress, 1994.

IV. Movement 1

Philippians 2:5-11—
The Drama of Christ's
Humiliation and Exaltation

A. Translation and Structural Analysis

    5 Regard one another according to the pattern founded on Christ
      Jesus,

[1] 6 Who, though he was of divine status,
      did not regard being like God
      something to take selfish advantage of.

[2] 7 Rather he made himself powerless,
      assuming a slave's status,
      being born as a human being.
[3]   And while existing in human appearance,

    8 he further humbled himself
      by being obedient unto death,
      even death by crucifixion.

[4] 9 Wherefore God highly exalted him
      and bestowed upon him the name
      which is above every name,

[5] 10 so that at the name of Jesus
      every knee should bend
      of those in heaven, on earth, and under the earth;

[6] 11 and every tongue should confess
   that Jesus Christ is LORD
   to the glory of God the Father (personal paraphrase of NAB).

Before beginning my analysis proper of this hymn, I make two preliminary observations. First, because recent discussion of this Christological hymn has focused on the importance of the hymn's context for interpreting the hymn, I have included Philippians 2:5 from the hymn's immediate context in my adaptation of the NAB translation. Second, Peter T. O'Brien informs us that Johannes Weiss in 1897 was the first scholar in modern times "to detect the poetic, rhythmic nature" of Philippians 2:6-11; and that Ernst Lohmeyer in 1928 was the first to subject the hymn to a thorough-going analysis (1991, 189). This latter observation reminds us that detailed and scientific study of New Testament hymns is not a new phenomenon.

In the left margins I have used brackets to indicate the structure I detect in the hymn. It has six stanzas. In five of six, the beginning of a stanza accords with the beginning of a verse. Stanza three is the exception, for it begins at the end of verse seven and before the beginning of verse eight.

The hymn falls neatly into two major parts. Stanzas one through three sing of Christ Jesus' humbling of himself. Stanzas four through six give voice to God's exaltation of Christ Jesus. Thus, Christ Jesus is the subject of the first three stanzas, and God is the subject of the final three stanzas. And with one important exception each stanza has three lines.

I find it helpful to think that the basic pattern behind the hymn is the divine principle found on Jesus' lips in Matthew 23:12, Luke 14:11, and Luke 18:14. I quote from Luke 14:11: "For everyone who exalts himself will be humbled, but the one who humbles himself will be exalted." The Greek words translated "humbles himself" in Luke 14:11 are at root the same ones used in the translation, "humbled himself," in stanza three of Philippians 2:6-11. And the verb "exalts" in Luke 14:11 forms the basic root of the verb, "highly exalted," found in stanza four of Philippians 2:6-11.

The composer has theologically and artistically expanded this divine principle of humiliation/exaltation in the two parts of the hymn. In what might be called complementary parallelism the composer has used a number of different ways in stanzas two and three to utter the truth that Christ Jesus humbled himself by becoming human. I call my readers' attention particularly to the clauses which begin with "assuming," "being born," and "existing" in stanzas two and three. Behind each of these words is a Greek participle, not a finite verb. And the content of the clauses which commence with a participle say about the same thing and complement one another: Christ Jesus humbled himself by becoming a real human being. The composer has highlighted the nadir of this humiliation by assigning the words "even death by crucifixion" to a special line, which seems to break the symmetry of six stanzas with three lines each. When we turn to an analysis of part two of the hymn, we notice that stanzas five and six expand or complement, through the use of finite forms of the Greek verb, what has just been sung in stanza four, namely God's exaltation of Christ Jesus.

Happily, the composer of the six stanzas of Philippians 2:6-11 believed that women and men do not live by principles alone, but by stories and dramas which give foundational meaning to the principle and exemplify it. Indeed, our theology and our piety would be impoverished if we lacked the composer's insistence upon the submission of "every knee" and the confession of "every tongue" at the mention of Jesus' name. And how feeble our understanding of Christ Jesus would be if we lacked stanza two of the hymn and were reduced to the simple principle of stanza three: "he humbled himself"!

For the interested reader, I make a methodological point about the detection of a structure in the hymn of Philippians 2:6-11. In discovering this structure of six stanzas, I take with utmost seriousness the caution of Morna D. Hooker (1975, 158–59) and other scholars, that the structure which scholars perceive in the hymn must not determine the meaning of the hymn's content or determine what additions Paul might have made to correct the theology of the original hymn. To give a concrete example, Werner Stenger argues that Philippians 2:6-11 has a certain structural consistency. Then he determines that three lines do not conform to this structure, namely, "taking the form of a servant," "even death on a cross," and "to the glory of God the Father." In his opinion these lines "destroy the structural consistency of the text and must be viewed as later additions of the author who is citing the hymn, namely, Paul. If we read the text without these additions, the parallelism between the text's components and their macrostructural arrangement are easily discernible and give the text the character of a consciously formed poetic text" (1993, 120). How can Stenger be so certain that he has detected the true form of the hymn and thus sure that Paul has made additions to or corrections of this putatively original hymn?

If I leave Stenger's analysis to one side, I can approach the methodological point I am stressing from another angle, one that I have already broached in my analysis earlier of the exceptional fourth line of stanza three. One cannot legitimately argue that because the third stanza has four lines whereas all the other stanzas have three lines that Paul must have corrected the Christology of the original hymn by adding line four to the third stanza: "even death by crucifixion." I will keep the hymn intact and will argue later that the composer uses the so-called exception of the fourth line of the third stanza as a literary device to highlight the extent to which Christ Jesus became a slave (second stanza) and to anticipate the wonder of God's exaltation of this crucified slave to be universal Lord (fifth and sixth stanzas).

I offer two additional reasons for keeping the hymn intact. Charles H. Talbert, who also maintains that the hymn of Philippians 2:6-11 is integral (1967), reminded me in a recent conversation that artists in antiquity shied away from perfect symmetry, for they considered it imperfect. In such a world the nonsymmetry of a given stanza would be perfect. Second, I find a distant, but evocative parallel in the hymnic libretto which Picander, aka Christian Friedrich Henrici, composed for J. S. Bach's "St. Matthew's Passion." In at least three recitations (1, 39, and 51) Picander, the master of balanced verses and intricate rhymes, forsook his craft to accentuate God's mercy. Particularly instructive is recitative fifty-one on "The Scourging of Jesus," which has an odd number of lines, not the usual even number of lines. And in Picander's rhyming scheme, line one is exceptional, for it is unrhymed and thereby highlighted: "Erbaum es Gott!" (O merciful God!). I am quick to grant that Picander is not the composer of

Philippians 2:6-11 and that he worked in the eighteenth century, not the first. My point is simple: there is a basis in musical composition for the position I espouse, that "even death by crucifixion" is not redactional but an integral part of the hymn.

In conclusion, I openly confess that the points I have raised are exciting in their speculation and potentially very significant theologically. For example, if Stenger's analysis is correct, then we have concrete proof that Paul corrected a Gnostic redeemer myth which had become part of the worship service of many early Christian communities and which was in danger of proclaiming a Christ Jesus who did not become genuinely human and whose exaltation was to the diminishment of the glory of God the Father (1993, 121–22).

B. THE CONTEXT

Before discussing the immediate and broader context of our hymn, let me share my assumptions about Philippians. I am persuaded, by those who study ancient epistolography, that Philippians is a letter of friendship and is integral. That is, I do not consider Philippians 3:2-21 and 4:10-20 to be fragments of separate letters. Further, I accept as a given that Paul authors his friendship letter to the Philippians to foster a greater unity among them. As Ben Witherington writes: "What unifies this letter is the appeal to unity and the arguments against a variety of problems both internal and external that threaten to undo that unity" (1994, 57). In the annotated bibliography at the end of this chapter I make reference to studies which give detailed arguments to support my presuppositions.

Philippians 2:2-5 and 2:12 are vitally important for interpreting the *immediate context* of the hymn in Philippians 2:6-11. I treat 2:12 first. From the inferential word "so then," which commences 2:12, it is easy to see that Paul quotes the hymn of 2:6-11 to influence the conduct of the Philippians: "*So then*, my beloved, obedient as you have always been, not only when I am present but all the more now that I am absent, work out your salvation with fear and trembling" (italics mine). But it is only when we turn to 2:2-5 that we see what conduct Paul is trying to persuade the Philippians to adopt. And we should not be surprised to see that Paul's concern is about unity.

In the following, I quote the NRSV translation of Philippians 2:2-5, italicize some key words, and ask my readers to see whether any of the terminology or thoughts of 2:2-5 are picked up and developed by the hymn of 2:6-11:

> (2) . . . make my joy complete: *be of the same mind,* having the same love, being in full accord and *of one mind.* (3) Do nothing from selfish ambition or conceit, but *in humility regard* others as better than yourselves. (4) Let each of you look not to your own interests, but to the interests of others. (5) Let *the same mind* be in you that was in Christ Jesus . . . .

I would suggest that 2:2-5 points ahead quite explicitly to stanzas one through three of the hymn of 2:6-11, for stanzas one through three accentuate the thoughts of Christ Jesus, who "did not *regard* being like God something to take selfish advantage of" (stanza one) and who was "obedient unto death" (stanza three). See also the action of Christ Jesus portrayed in stanza three, "he further *humbled* himself," which has been anticipated in 2:3: "but *in humility* regard others as better than yourselves."

With the evidence in hand of similar terminology in both 2:2-5 and 2:6-8, we can appreciate the argument that some scholars make that the hymn of 2:6-11 is used by Paul to show Christ Jesus as an ethical example to the Philippians. That is, if the Philippians would only follow the example of the self-sacrificing Christ Jesus, there would be greater unity among them. While this argument is helpful and spiritually challenging, it needs to be supplemented by another line of thought to show how Christ Jesus' exaltation (stanzas four through six) is also interpreted by the immediate context of 2:2-5. For surely Christians' imitation of Christ Jesus comes to an insurmountable barrier when we consider that Christ Jesus was exalted by God. That's not in store for us Christians, no matter how perfectly we imitate the humiliation of Christ Jesus, or is it? (See my discussion later on the total context of Philippians, especially on 3:20-21.)

The observations of Wayne Meeks are helpful because they suggest how stanzas four through six fit the context of 2:2-5. Meeks argues that all of 2:6-11 should be seen as a drama which creates community. That is, all six stanzas contribute to the creation of unity among the Philippians, not just the first three, and they do so as a story. While very important, Meeks' observations need greater exemplification. Again, allow me to use an in-house Franciscan example: the story of St. Francis of Assisi and the lepers. I quote from the beginning of *The Testament of St. Francis:* "This is how God inspired me, Brother Francis, to embark upon a life of penance. When I was in sin, the sight of lepers nauseated me beyond measure; but then God himself led me into their company, and I had pity on them. When I had once become acquainted with them, what had previously nauseated me became a source of spiritual and physical consolation for me. After that I did not wait long before leaving the world" (Habig 1973, 67).

No number of novitiates, no volume of legislation, and no commands from superiors have created the Franciscan love and care for the poor. Rather, it has been the simple story of Francis of Assisi and the lepers, read in a society dominated by care of the marginalized, which has created communities of Franciscan men and women dedicated to serving the poor. Contemporary Franciscans don't examine their consciences so much according to whether they have observed the norms of poverty found in *General Constitutions* (1988) and *General Statutes* (1992), but rather according to whether they have actualized the story of Francis and the lepers in their lives.

I'm sure that in your own family there are stories which have helped create who you are and explain why you celebrate Thanksgiving or Christmas the way you do. Then there are the stories of the founding mothers and fathers which create the country and citizens of the United States, are celebrated on the Fourth of July and other national holidays, and are commemorated by such pilgrim attractions as Boston's Freedom Trail. These stories, as well as the story of Francis of Assisi and the lepers, are . similar to the story found in Philippians 2:6-11. They create and continue to create communities. But there is one big difference. We have the life of Christ Jesus abiding among us as we strive to create our Christian community. Indeed, that's the importance of the phrase found at the end of Philippians 2:5—"in Christ Jesus." Our imitation of Christ Jesus' self-sacrifice is not done by ourselves alone. It is done under the power of that same Christ Jesus who has been exalted to be cosmic Lord over those powers which might impede us from imitating his example of humble service. I conclude my discussion of the critical point that Philippians 2:6-11 is a soteriological story by accentuating the cardinal role of faith. It takes an act of faith to make Christ Jesus' story in 2:6-11 normative for me. Similarly, at some point in their training Franciscans must invest authority or believe in the story of Francis and the lepers. Otherwise, that story will be just another story and will not become the lodestar of their lives.

In the *broader context* of the hymn, the main verses are 3:20-21, which are closely related to stanzas four through six of our hymn. I quote from the NRSV and underline key words: (20) "But our citizenship is in heaven, and it is from there that we are expecting a Savior, the Lord Jesus Christ. (21) He will transform the body of our *humiliation* that it may be conformed to the body of his glory, *by the power that also enables him to make all things subject to himself.*" There is an obvious play on the same basic Greek root in 2:3 ("in humility"), 2:8 ("he humbled himself"), and 3:21 ("body of our humiliation"). But the main correspondence is between 2:2-5, 2:9-11, and 3:21: If Christians humble themselves (2:2-5), then Christ Jesus will use the power which God has given to him (2:9-11) for their benefit (3:21). Put in different words, 3:21 gives us the key to unlock the full mystery of how stanzas four through six relate to the immediate context of 2:6-11. Indeed, we cannot imitate God's exaltation of Jesus, but Christ Jesus will use the power bestowed on him through God's exaltation to benefit those who have humbled themselves in imitation of him. Let me highlight this mystery from another angle. Because of the parallel passage of 3:21 we now know more of the import of the drama of 2:6-11 and realize that this drama is not just Christ Jesus'. It is also ours as we, who are humbling ourselves in imitation of Christ Jesus, await our Savior who will transform us. Perhaps no one has expressed the important interpretive relationship between the context and hymn of 2:6-11 more eloquently than Morna D. Hooker:

> In becoming what we are, Christ becomes subject to human frustrations and enslavement to hostile powers; but his very action in becoming what we are is a demonstration of what he eternally is— ungrasping, unself-centred, giving glory by all his actions to God. It

is because of this paradox, the absurdity of the form of God being demonstrated in the form of a slave, that Christians can become like Christ; it is because God's glory is demonstrated in shame and weakness (as Paul puts it elsewhere) that at one and the same time Paul can tell the Philippians to be like Christ in his action of *humiliation* and promise them that Christ will transform their bodies of *humiliation* to be like his own glorious body (1975, 164).

I conclude this section on context by anticipating my later reflection starters. While it is the challenge of a lifetime to imitate Christ Jesus, who rendered himself powerless, I am convinced that the greater challenge is to believe the good news that Jesus Christ has become cosmic Lord and has the power to transform our body of humiliation to be like his glorious body. Can we and dare we allow the drama of Philippians 2:6-11 to shape our lives? Expressed in terms of the drama of Francis of Assisi and the lepers, can we believe that through genuine contact with life's wretchedness we will receive conversion, new light, and new life?

C. Key Concepts and Images

The key concepts and images of Philippians 2:6-11 are so numerous, that I will be selective in my treatment. The major analogy I employ in presenting these selected concepts and images is that of a piece of music which subtly incorporates into itself older material. For my analogy I use Aaron Copland's *Billy the Kid.* Into his musical composition Copland has incorporated the melodies of such cowboy songs as "Git Along Little Doggies," "Streets of Laredo," "The Old Chisholm Trail," and "Oh Bury Me Not On The Lone Prairie," and done so in such a masterful way that they all blend into the new creation. As a matter of fact, if you are not familiar with the old cowboy songs you may well not be aware that Copland is even quoting from them. And even if you are familiar with these songs from America's west, you may not recognize them at the first listening of *Billy the Kid* because Copland does not devote much time to them.

If I apply the analogy of what Copland has done in composing *Billy the Kid* to Philippians 2:6-11, I make the following observations preliminary to my discussion of that hymn's key concepts and images. First, the composer of 2:6-11, while creative, did not create the hymn without any background whatsoever. Second, scholars have discovered various backgrounds for the key concepts and images of the hymn, finding these backgrounds especially in the Old Testament. Third, because of our unfamiliarity with the Old Testament, particularly in its Greek version which was used by New Testament authors, we may not see an Old Testament reference the first time we read the hymn. Finally, like with the old television quiz show, we may marvel that someone can "name that tune" (i.e., find an Old Testament reference) by hearing one or two "notes," e.g., the note *slave* in stanza one or *obedient* in stanza three.

With the above music lesson in mind, let's explore the hymn of Philippians 2:6-11 to see where and how the composer has incorporated previous Old Testament tunes. I limit myself to four key concepts and images: preexistence, slavery, the obedience of the new Adam, and exaltation. In an advanced music lesson on Philippians 2:6-11 other themes could be examined and enjoyed.

It can be well argued that Christ Jesus' *preexistence* is presupposed throughout stanzas one through three. That is, the *who* of whom the hymn sings in its first ten lines existed before "assuming a slave's status." In other words, Christ Jesus' divine status preexists his "slave status." Since we are talking about technical terms, I give a more precise definition of preexistence: "By 'preexistence' we mean that before Jesus' birth or earthly appearance—indeed, even before creation—he resided with God as the 'Son of God,' as the 'word' *(logos)*, or in the 'manner of divine existence'; God even created the world 'in him' ('mediator of creation') in order to send him into the world in the end time" (Stenger 1993, 129). Stenger's definition is comprehensive and uses examples from various New Testament writings. *Son of God* is the term for preexistence used in Romans 1:3-4 and John 3:16-17. *Word* is the term for preexistence in the prologue of John's Gospel. By "manner of divine existence" Stenger refers to stanza one of our hymn. Finally, "in him" ("mediator of creation") points to verse sixteen of the hymn in Colossians 1:15-20.

If one asks about the Old Testament background for the theme of preexistence which runs through stanzas one through three, I recall Proverbs 8:22-31 and quote some salient verses: "When the Lord established the heavens, I [Wisdom] was there. . . . When he marked out the foundations of the earth, then I was beside him, like a master worker; and I was daily his delight, rejoicing before him always, rejoicing in his inhabited world and delighting in the human race" (8:27-31, NRSV). Stenger (1993, 130) cites the Book of Wisdom 9:9-10 as apt background: "Now with you is Wisdom, who knows your works and was present when you made the world; who understands what is pleasing in your eye and what is conformable with your commands. Send her forth from your holy heavens and from your glorious throne dispatch her, that she may be with me and work with me, that I may know what is your pleasure."

If we accept passages like Proverbs 8:22-31 and Wisdom 9:9-10 as background from which to understand stanzas one through three of Philippians 2:6-11, then we catch sight of what these stanzas reveal about God. The power, wisdom, and creative love and delight of God are revealed in Christ Jesus who made himself powerless, was a slave, lived a human life, and was crucified. Or to quote from Morna Hooker again, Christ Jesus' "very action in becoming what we are is a demonstration of what he eternally is—ungrasping, unself-centred. . . ." (1975, 164). Such a revelation is truly salvific, liberating us from our self-focused existence.

Discerning the tune of preexistence in this hymn may not be as easy as spotting the melody of the song "Oh Bury Me Not On The Lone Prairie" in Copland's *Billy the Kid* because of our unfamiliarity with passages like Proverbs 8:22-31 and Wisdom 9:9-10. But now that you have learned the melody of Proverbs and Wisdom, might you hear them being played in stanzas one through three of Philippians 2:6-11?

Now that your ears are attuned to hear some of the melodies in the hymn of Philippians 2:6-11, let me direct your attention to the melody behind *slave* in the phrase "assuming a slave's status" in stanza two. There are three candidates for the melody behind *slave* in stanza two. The first background is popularly known through the suffering servant song of Isaiah 52:13–53:12. In the Septuagint (Greek translation of these materials) the word *humiliation* occurs in 53:8. If you recall, the same Greek stem stands behind the verb "he *humbled* himself" in stanza three of Philippians 2:6-11. But more importantly it may be argued that behind the expression "he made himself powerless" of stanza two stands Isaiah 53:12: "he surrendered himself to death."

How are we to evaluate this background for *slave* in stanza two? On the positive side, it must be acknowledged that Christian tradition, beginning with the New Testament in such passages as 1 Peter 2:22-25 and the accounts of the institution of the Eucharist, has used Isaiah 52:13–53:12 to interpret how Jesus' death has taken away our sins. Yet this Isaiah passage does not seem to lie behind Philippians 2:6-11 for the following reasons. First, it uses *servant,* not *slave.* Second, the Greek text of Isaiah 53:12 does not match the Greek text in Philippians: "he made himself powerless" (stanza two). Finally, even if there were a closer match between the Greek of Isaiah 53:12 and Philippians 2:7, then we would have to face the problem of chronological incongruity created in the hymn by such an interpretation. That is, stanza two would present Christ Jesus dying before stanza three describes his death.

Even though it seems that the suffering servant song of Isaiah does not stand directly behind *slave* in Philippians, it may very well be that Isaiah's suffering servant has become the historical and theological model behind the next contender to claim that it provides the religious interpretive background for *slave.*

A second interpretation of *slave* comes from the tradition of God's vindication of the righteous who have suffered and given up their lives to be obedient to God's will as found in the law. Thus, this interpretation would not only explain *slave* in stanza two, but would also shed light on the vindication motif in stanzas four through six. Wisdom 2–5 is usually cited as background for this attractive interpretation, but the author of Wisdom does not refer to the righteous who are faithful to and vindicated by God as *slaves.* Indeed, the suffering righteous of 2 Maccabees are referred to as *slaves* of God, but only once: "Though our living Lord treats us harshly for a little while to correct us with chastisements, he will again be reconciled with his *slaves*" (italics mine—2 Macc 7:33, NAB adapted).

I make two points about the third and final interpretation of *slave.* One is based on the general first-century perception of what it meant to be a human being. That is, to be human was to be subject to hostile powers. In my chapter on backgrounds I give some indication of the pervasiveness of this conviction under the rubric of "an age of anxiety." Seen from this historical angle, Christ Jesus' incarnation meant becoming a slave to these hostile powers.

Besides this historical background, I bring the witness of the Pauline tradition to bear on this interpretation of *slave* as being subject to hostile powers. In Galatians Paul spends all of chapter four trying to convince his Galatian converts that they have been freed by Christ Jesus from slavery to the hostile powers. Galatians 4:8-9 is particularly instructive: "At a time when you did not know God, you became *slaves* to things that by nature are not gods; but now that you have come to know God, or rather to be known by God, how can you turn back again to the weak and destitute elemental powers? Do you want to be *slaves* to them all over again?" (italics mine). In Romans 8:15 Paul again alludes to the freedom from slavery which Christians have received and adds the point that the Spirit has effected this freedom: "For you did not receive a spirit of *slavery* to fall back into fear, but you received a spirit of adoption, through which we cry, *Abba,* 'Father!'" (italics mine). Finally, Colossians 2:8 also refers to these hostile powers which strive to enslave women and men: "See to it that no one captivate you with an empty, seductive philosophy according to human tradition, according to the elemental powers of the world and not according to Christ." (See the chapter on the hymn of Colossians 1:15-20 for more detail on these "elemental powers of the world.") In sum, Paul himself, in his major epistles—Romans and Galatians—provides cogent evidence on how the word *slave* might be interpreted in a hymn which circulated in one of his communities: to be human is to be in thralldom to hostile powers, and to be saved is to be liberated from slavery to these same hostile powers.

Granted this Pauline interpretation of slave, we find some concord with it in stanza five of Philippians 2:6-11: "so that at the name of Jesus every knee should bend *of those in heaven, on earth, and under the earth*" (italics mine). As we will see in greater detail below in my fourth "Key Concepts and Images," Christ Jesus, who submitted to the hostile powers, has now been vindicated by God. Now, as cosmic Lord, Christ Jesus rules over such hostile powers wherever they may be. Further, when Christ Jesus was at his lowest point, enduring the punishment of crucifixion which was meted out to slaves, God exalted him over those powers whose intent is to enslave.

Who would have thought that there could be so many possible "melodies" behind the simple and single word *slave* in our composer's hymn? While I think that there is more and clearer evidence for the third interpretation, I do not look askance at those who hum the melody of either the first or second interpretation. (Interested readers may check my chapter on Ephesians 2:14-16 for a fuller explanation of the role of ambiguity in hymns.)

Perhaps, we have become so used to reading or hearing that Christ Jesus was obedient to the point of death (stanza three) that we no longer ask why the composer chose to use the word *obedience* in the first place. I will explore the background melody of the word *obedience* in order to mention, albeit very briefly, the position of those who interpret stanzas one through three as the story of Christ Jesus, the new Adam, who did not selfishly hold onto the divine image, his likeness to God, and who was fully human and fully obedient to God to the lowest point of his life—death by crucifixion.

Introducing such a background as the new Adam may seem to have no basis whatsoever in the word *obedience* of stanza three until we realize that twice, in major sections of his theology, Paul contrasts Christ Jesus, the new Adam, with the old Adam. While Paul develops the contrast at length in Romans 5:12-21, 5:19 will be sufficient for our purposes: "For just as through the *disobedience* of one person the many were made sinners, so through the *obedience* of one the many will be made righteous" (italics mine). (It should be noted that the Greek word which lies behind *obedience* is the same basic Greek word/root which lies behind the adjective obedient in stanza three of Philippians 2:6-11). In Paul's theology *disobedience* characterizes the old Adam. *Obedience* is characteristic of the new Adam. And in 1 Corinthians 15:45-49, Paul contrasts the two Adams to make a vital point about the resurrection of believers. I quote from the opening and concluding verses of this passage: "So, too, it is written, 'The first man, Adam, became a living being,' the last Adam a life-giving spirit. . . . Just as we have borne the image of the earthly one, we shall also bear the image of the heavenly one." Among the points that Paul makes in

1 Corinthians 15:45-49 is that the new or last Adam is a life-giving spirit. Presupposed, it seems to me, are the new Adam's *obedience* (as found in Rom 5:19) and his own resurrection (see Rom 1:4). At this point it seems wise to direct readers interested in finding more parallels between Genesis 1–3 and Philippians 2:6-11, to the works of O'Brien (1991) and Hooker (1975). These authors argue that the Greek *morphe* behind "divine status" in stanza one of Philippians 2:6-11 means the same as the Greek *eikon* which is usually translated "image" in Genesis 1:26: "Then God said, 'Let us make humankind in our *image*'" (NRSV). Further, a case will be made that behind "being like God" of stanza one of Philippians 2:6-11 lies Genesis 3:4-5: "But the serpent said to the woman, 'you will not die; for God knows that when you eat of it (the tree) your eyes will be opened, and you will *be like God*'" (italics mine, NRSV). While it remains doubtful that one can sustain many detailed parallels between the story of the first Adam in Genesis 1–3 and the story of the new Adam in stanzas one through three of our hymn, the general parallel is persuasive. That is, the disobedience, arrogance, and self-aggrandizement of the first Adam are contrasted with the obedience, humility, and self-lessness of the second Adam.

In conclusion, I share my conviction that the figure of the obedient new Adam, Christ Jesus, goes a long way in providing the melody which is to be heard behind "being obedient unto death" in stanza three. People like the Philippians, evangelized and educated by Paul, are presumed to have heard such a melody in a hymn circulated in Pauline circles. Whether they heard other New Adam music is a highly contested point.

My fourth and final key concept and image is *exaltation.* In considering my treatment of the first three key concepts and images, you may have thought that your hearing was failing; for you had a hard time hearing the melodies behind *preexistence, slave,* and *obedience.* To use the analogy from Copland's *Billy the Kid* again, you thought you would never hear the melody of the song, "Oh Bury Me Not On The Lone Prairie" in Copland's ballet because it was sounded for such a short time. Almost as a reward for your perseverance in listening intently for the melodies behind the first three key concepts and images, the composer devotes

more time to the melody behind *exaltation* in stanzas four
through six. The melody finds voice in Isaiah 45:22-25, which
proclaims the absolute sovereignty of God and promises vindication for God's people:

> 22 Turn to me and be safe,
>   all you ends of the earth,
>   for I am God; there is no other!
> 23 By myself I swear,
>   uttering my just decree
>   and my unalterable word:
>   *To me every knee shall bend;*
>   *by me every tongue shall swear,*
> 24 Saying, "only in the Lord
>   are just deeds and power.
>   Before him in shame shall come
>   all who vent their anger against him.
> 25 In the Lord shall be the vindication and the glory
>   of all the descendants of Israel (italics mine, NAB).

The italicized lines are key to the melody being quoted in stanzas
four through six. Indeed, God has given Christ Jesus his own
name, Lord. And at the mention of this new name every knee and
every tongue shall be submissive to Christ Jesus. At this juncture I
remind my readers that in my discussion of the background of
slave, I highly recommended the opinion that *slave* referred to
Christ Jesus' human status of being submissive to the hostile powers. In the divine reversal of humiliation/exaltation, sung in stanzas four through six of our hymn, Christ Jesus is now Lord, and
Lord, too, over these hostile powers. For the universal authority of
Christ Jesus, the Lord, is over all hostile powers wherever they
exist, be it "in heaven, on earth, and under the earth" (stanza five).

I conclude this lengthy section on key concepts and images
with a small dose of pedagogical prescription. If you try to hear at
the same time all the four melodies behind Philippians 2:6-11,
you may be overwhelmed and frustrated. Try the procedure that I
often recommend to those who want to study the Gospels: take
one idea or theme, e.g., food, and read all twenty-four chapters of
Luke's Gospel from that perspective. I give the same prescription
for reading Philippians 2:6-11. First, read it from the perspective

of *preexistence,* then *slave,* next *obedience,* and finally *exaltation.* I wish you happy and spiritually uplifting viewing and listening!

D. REFLECTION STARTERS

To begin these reflections, I return to the notion that *the hymn of Philippians 2:6-11 is a drama or story,* and consider how it may be heard by various age groups. In their idealism, enthusiasm, and altruism the young will more easily accept the story of Philippians 2:6-11, especially stanzas one through three about self-denial. For the old, stanzas four through six may make more sense as they struggle to find meaning in their experience of increasing diminishment. In nurturing this reflection, I have been aided by an interview which the celebrated Roman Catholic theologian Karl Rahner gave when he was in the winter of his life: "Young people often attempt to commit themselves to things from which per se they do not hope to gain anything for themselves. All these are spontaneous, indeed positive, joyous, and inspiring experiences. . . . And so an old person (also) has a natural access to God coming out of his or her positive experience of the world. But, more often than not, one probably will encounter the negative side in an old person. Generally people do not die in an ecstasy of enthusiasm and joy, but rather with difficulty and apparently in a melancholy draining away of life" (Imhof 1990, 110.)

For old people, who have given of themselves for others, Philippians 2:6-11, especially stanzas four through six, make good spiritual sense. And if we link those last three stanzas together with 3:20-21 as we advised earlier, then we know for sure, in faith, that our universal Lord, Christ Jesus, will transform our corruptible body, constantly subject to diminishment, to be like his incorruptible and glorious body.

Perhaps this is all a bit too theoretical. I leave the clouds and touch the earth in my second reflection. Whether old or young, all of us can learn about the deep meaning of Philippians 2:6-11 from the life of Dorothy Day (1897–1980), cofounder of the Catholic Worker Movement. At age seventy-five she did not hold selfishly to her freedom, but willingly suffered imprisonment to help vindicate the marginalized. Besides engaging in bold action for the liberation of the downtrodden, Dorothy Day lived with them daily. Daily, too, she nurtured her union with God through the Catholic piety of Mass, rosary, and two hours of meditation, especially on Scripture. And as Robert Coles tells us from his interviews with her, Philippians 2 was frequently the subject of her meditation. In terms of the theme of this chapter, Dorothy Day let the drama of Philippians 2:6-11 form her life as she daily struggled to live the common life at the New York Catholic Worker house, sharing with others, being obedient to their needs, trying to be at one with all (Coles 1987, 132–33). And as thousands of people throughout the United States now refer to her as Saint Dorothy Day, one realizes that women and men from different Christian traditions have seen and acknowledged Christ's image profoundly alive in her—humiliated with the humiliated, but now exalted by God.

A third reflection deals with *contextualization*. Let's extract the hymn from its context in Philippians, thus leading our thoughts away from the hymn's message of Christ Jesus as a model to be imitated and directing our attention to the worship of Christ Jesus, our universal Lord. This seems to be the way in which the Roman Catholic Liturgy of the Hours uses the hymn as it assigns it to first vespers for all four Sundays. The church gathered at prayer is not so much exhorted to follow the humility of Christ Jesus, as it is to praise Christ Jesus who has been given God's very own name of Lord. Thus, those at prayer add their own tongues to the chorus of those who worship Christ Jesus, universal Lord. On the other hand, in its use of Philippians 2:6-11 as the standard second reading for Palm Sunday the Roman Catholic liturgy contextualizes the hymn in such a way that the congregation is drawn to reflect on how it should imitate the innocently suffering righteous one, Jesus of Nazareth, the account of whose passion follows as the Gospel text for Palm Sunday. Further, Philippians 2:6-11 is set in an extraordinary context during the Liturgy of the Word on Good Friday as the humiliation/exaltation of Christ Jesus found in 2:8-9 becomes the canticle sung before the reading of John's passion account. It is to be recalled here that John's passion account accentuates Jesus' glorification so much as to almost eliminate Jesus' humiliation. Finally, we might ask what new

transformations of meaning 2:6-11 undergoes as it is incorporated into the contexts of hymns which the Christian community
sings during different celebrations.
My final reflection underscores *Christ Jesus' lordship over the
hostile powers.* Christ Jesus, our universal Lord, is in control of all
those hostile powers which would turn us away from God as we
endeavor to lead our Christian lives in our own age of anxiety.
Horoscope and fate, rabbit's foot and black cat's path, evil eye and
voodoo doll do not dominate our days. We journey in faith, confident in the power of our universal Lord, finding meaning for the
present and hope for the future in the story sung forth in
Philippians 2:6-11.

ANNOTATED BIBLIOGRAPHY

Byrne, Brendan. "The Letter to the Philippians." *The New Jerome
    Biblical Commentary.* Eds. Raymond E. Brown, Joseph A. Fitzmyer,
    and Roland E. Murphy, 48:18–22. Englewood Cliffs: Prentice Hall,
    1990. This is an excellent and accessible treatment of the complex-
    ities and theological riches of Philippians 2:6-11.
Coles, Robert. *Dorothy Day: A Radical Devotion.* Radcliffe Biography
    Series. Reading: Addison-Wesley, 1987.
Fowl, Stephen E. *The Story of Christ in the Ethics of Paul: An Analysis of
    the Function of the Hymnic Material in the Pauline Corpus.* Journal for
    the Study of the New Testament Supplement Series 36, 77–101.
    Sheffield: JSOT Press, 1990. A helpful attempt to show how
    Philippians 2:6-11 is related to its context.
*The General Statutes of the Order of Friars Minor: Our Plan for Franciscan
    Living.* Pulaski: Franciscan Publishers, 1992. This English transla-
    tion of the General Statutes contains 237 articles and is published
    by The Franciscan O.F.M. Conference of North America.
Habig, Marion A., ed. *St. Francis of Assisi, Writings and Early Biographies:
    English Omnibus of the Sources for the Life of St. Francis.* Chicago:
    Franciscan Herald Press, 1973.
Hooker, Morna D. "Philippians 2:6-11," *Jesus und Paulus: Festschrift für
    Werner Georg Kümmel zum 70. Geburtstag.* Eds. E. Earle Ellis and
    Erich Graesser, 151–64. Göttingen: Vandenhoeck and Ruprecht,
    1975. A learned and inspiring article on the structure and back-
    ground of Philippians 2:6-11.

Imhof, Paul, and Hubert Biallowons, eds. *Faith in a Wintry Season: Conversations and Interviews with Karl Rahner in the Last Years of His Life.* New York: Crossroad, 1990.

Martin, Ralph P. *Carmen Christi: Philippians ii.5-11 in Recent Interpretation and in the Setting of Early Christian Worship.* Rev. ed. Grand Rapids: Eerdmans, 1983. The original of this thorough and scholarly monograph was published in 1967.

Meeks, Wayne A. "The Man from Heaven in Paul's Letter to the Philippians." *The Future of Early Christianity: Essays in Honor of Helmut Koester.* Ed. Birger A. Pearson, 329–36. Minneapolis: Fortress, 1991. Meeks argues persuasively that Philippians 2:6-11 is a drama which creates Christian community.

O'Brien, Peter T. *The Epistle to the Philippians: A Commentary on the Greek Text.* The New International Greek Testament Commentary. Grand Rapids: Eerdmans, 1991. O'Brien devotes pp. 186–271 to Philippians 2:6-11 and gives excellent summaries of many of the ninety-seven or so items he provides in his bibliography. A treasure trove of information for the advanced student. I have learned much at the feet of Professor O'Brien.

The Rule and the General Constitutions of the Order of Friars Minor: Our Plan for Franciscan Living. Pulaski: Franciscan Publishers, 1988. This English translation of the General Constitutions contains 261 articles and is published by The Franciscan O.F.M. Conference of North America.

Stenger, Werner. *Introduction to New Testament Exegesis,* 118–22, 129–32. Grand Rapids: Eerdmans, 1993. One of the few contemporary New Testament introductions which devotes a chapter to New Testament hymns and uses Philippians 2:6-11 and 1 Timothy 3:16 as examples.

Talbert, Charles H. "The Problem of Pre-Existence in Philippians 2:6-11." *Journal of Biblical Literature* 86 (1967) 141–53. Talbert argues that Philippians 2:6-11 is unredacted and that its form reveals that it does not teach the preexistence of Jesus Christ.

White, L. Michael. "Morality Between Two Worlds: A Paradigm of Friendship in Philippians." *Greeks, Romans, and Christians: Essays in Honor of Abraham J. Malherbe.* Eds. David L. Balch, Everett Ferguson, and Wayne A. Meeks, 201–15. Minneapolis: Fortress, 1990. Excellent treatment of Philippians as an integral letter of friendship and of the function of the "soteriological drama" of Philippians 2:6-11 within the entire letter.

Witherington III, Ben. *Friendship and Finances in Philippi: The Letter of Paul to the Philippians.* The New Testament in Context. Valley

Forge: Trinity Press International, 1994. A popular treatment of contemporary scholarly views about the integrity and theology of Philippians. Considerable materials on how friendship and finances worked in first century Philippi and how Paul used these motifs in developing Philippians.

V. Movement 2

Colossians 1:15-20— Christ Jesus as Cosmic Lord and Peacemaker

A. Translation and Structural Analysis

15a   . . . Who is the image of the invisible God,

15b   the firstborn of *all* creation.

16a   For **in him** were created *all* things

16b   in heaven and on earth,

16c   the visible and the invisible,

16d   whether thrones or dominions

16e   whether principalities or powers;

16f   *all* things were created **through him** and **for him.**

17a   And he is before *all* things,

17b   and *all* things **in him** hold together.

18a   And he is the head of the body, the church.

18b   Who is the beginning, the firstborn from the dead,

18c   that in *all* things he himself might be preeminent.

19   For **in him** *all* the fullness was pleased to dwell,

20a   and **through him** to reconcile *all* things **for him,**

20b   making peace through the blood of his cross, **through him,**

20c   whether those on earth or those in heaven (italics mine, NAB adapted).

Before commencing my analysis of this majestic hymn, I offer two observations: one short and one lengthy. First, the scholarly literature on this hymn concerning its relationship to the polemic of Colossians 2 and its contemporary applications is massive. To do justice to the hymn and to its ancient and contemporary contexts, I will have to sample much scholarly literature and bring in technical arguments from time to time. Readers not interested in such discussions are advised to skip these scrumptious side dishes and to feast straightaway on the savory and succulent entree. In passing, I note that Eduard Norden in 1913 was the first scholar in modern times to identify "the undoubtedly old traditional material" of Colossians 1:15-20 (Martin 1973, 61).

Second, I must forewarn you that in my analysis of Colossians 1:15-20 I will be parting company with the scholarly consensus. Thus, I will not teach you that the author of Colossians redacted (corrected?) a hymn, highly regarded by him and the Colossians, by adding such words as "the church" in 1:18a and "through the blood of his cross" in 1:20b. But why would scholars see a redactor's pen at work at all? I enlist Ernst Käsemann as spokesperson for the scholarly majority. First, he argues that the hymn is composed of two parallel and antithetic stanzas (the same two stanzas I have proposed in my translation above), one dealing with creation and one with re-creation. Then he argues that the expression "the church" in 1:18a does not belong to the content of the first stanza which deals with creation seen almost from an ahistorical perspective, for "the church" is a theological term stemming from re-creation and is used to root creation in history. Next, Käsemann detects an exegetical stumbling block in 1:20b, for the "connexion of creation and eschatological new creation is broken by the reference to the event of the Cross—a reference for which the way is totally unprepared and which has immediately an anachronistic effect" (1964, 152). The reference to the cross also roots the theology of the hymn in everyday human existence. Käsemann provides some additional observations (1964, 150–52), but his main arguments are based on an analysis of style (two parallel and antithetic stanzas) and content (creation/re-creation).

How does one evaluate Käsemann's analysis and those like his? I make two methodological points. One is my own, and one is that of N. T. Wright. To me Käsemann's study of Colossians 1:15-20 is excellent in a New Testament classroom where philosophical and narrative logic reigns and dictates that creation must be separated from re-creation and the event of Jesus' death on the cross must be mentioned before the event of his resurrection from the dead. But hymns, and poetry in general, have a logic of their own, as our culture manifests in the phrase "poetic license," which the 1992 edition of *Random House Webster's College Dictionary* defines as "deviating from conventional form, logic, fact, etc., to produce a desired effect." Perhaps we scholars had better check our presuppositions about New Testament hymns: Do we assume that they must say everything about God and Jesus Christ and do so in the order of "salvation history"? Do we suppose that the New Testament hymns must follow the order we have detected, with the result that words like "the church" are seen as deviating from our order and therefore are additions?

If you press me for another example of New Testament "poetic license" in a hymn, I point to 1 Timothy 3:16:

> Who was manifested in the flesh,
> vindicated in the spirit,
> seen by angels,
> proclaimed to the Gentiles,
> believed in throughout the world,
> taken up in glory (NAB).

I refer my readers to my chapter on 1 Timothy 3:16 for a full treatment of this hymn about the universality of salvation. For our purposes, it is sufficient to note that the hymn almost defies the logic of the temporal sequence of salvation history to sing its Christology, for how can proclamation to the Gentiles and belief throughout the world occur before Jesus has ascended ("taken up in glory")? To my knowledge no scholar has seriously suggested that we eliminate a word from or add a word to 1 Timothy 3:16 so that it makes better chronological sense. Interpreters try their best to make sense of the hymn as it stands and do not resort to the speculation that an original hymn was redacted by the author of 1 Timothy. Interested readers can also check 1 Peter 3:22, which occurs at the end of a hymn which I discuss in another chapter of this book. This verse defies logic when its Greek text states that Jesus Christ sits at the right hand of God, has gone into heaven, with angels, authorities, and powers subject to him. In our way of thinking, first you enter a place and then you sit down. But that's not the logic of the author of this hymn. N. T. Wright finds fault with analyses like that of Käsemann on another level of method, as he employs a modern version of the *reductio ad absurdum* argument. If Käsemann can argue that the redactor added words to the hymn to have it make better theological sense, why can't some scholar argue that the redactor omitted words to have the hymn make better sense? Wright writes: ". . . if insertions are to be allowed omissions should be as well, making the task of reconstruction virtually impossible . . ." (1990, 445). I am in accord with Wright's conclusion: "The best way to proceed is to treat the passage, in the first instance, as it stands, and to see if it will yield satisfactory sense" (1990, 445). It will be the responsibility of my readers to see whether I have made satisfactory sense of the unredacted, integral hymn of Colossians 1:15-20.

Having completed my two initial observations, I turn to an analysis of the structure of Colossians 1:15-20, and do so by following the schema of Jean-Noël Aletti, who argues that it is composed of two stanzas and is unredacted. N. T. Wright has much the same schema, although he detects a chiasm (cross pattern) of A (1:15a-16f), B (1:17ab), B' (1:18a), and A' (1:18b-20c). Wright's chiastic structure may be an overrefinement. What is important is that Aletti, Wright, and I are members of a minority who maintain that Colossians 1:15-20 is composed of two stanzas; and what is even more important is that we maintain that the author of Colossians has not wielded a redactor's pen on this traditional hymn of two stanzas.

In the translation as I present it, I have highlighted other poetic features. I have italicized *all*, which occurs a total of eight times. There is a ninth time if you include 1:20c: "whether those on earth or those in heaven." As we will see later on, the hymn sings of the universal lordship and absolute primacy of Jesus Christ over all. No creature is excluded from his power.

I have put in boldfaced print the eight prepositional phrases where the composer of the hymn may have drawn upon popular philosophical tradition to indicate the primacy of Jesus Christ. In his power, through his power, and for the purpose God set forth through him is Jesus Christ supreme and preeminent. Eduard Lohse quotes Seneca to support his contention that "the final unity of all that exists is expressed by this succession of prepositions, which appears almost a play on words" (1971, 49 and no. 121). In *Epistle* 65,8 Seneca writes: "Accordingly, there are five causes, as Plato says: the one 'from which' (material), the one 'by which' (agent), the one 'in which' (formal), the one 'according to which' (exemplary), and the one 'for which' (final). Last comes the result of all these. Just as in the case of the statue . . . the one 'from which' is the bronze, the one 'by which' is the artist, the one 'in which' is the form which is adapted to it, the one 'according to which' is the pattern imitated by the maker, the one 'for which' is the purpose in the maker's mind, and, finally the result of all this is the statue itself." This same philosophical tradition is no stranger to the Pauline epistles, for it is also evidenced in 1 Corinthians 8:6: ". . . yet for us there is one God, the Father, from whom all things are and for whom we exist, and one Lord, Jesus Christ, through whom all things are and through whom we exist." Jesus Christ is not just one of five possible causes. He is all the causes.

Also, the composer has used various artistic parallels to construct the hymn. See, for example, how "the firstborn of all creation" (1:15b) of the first stanza corresponds to "the firstborn from the dead" (1:18b) at the beginning of the second stanza. As a matter of fact, this parallelism is one of the main reasons for separating Colossians 1:15-20 into two stanzas. Further, there is the clear parallelism, which is also chiastic, between 1:16b and 1:20c: heaven/earth—earth/heaven. More subtle is the chiastic parallel between 1:16a and 1:16f: "in him were created all things" (prepositional phrase, verb, *all things*) and "all things were created through him and for him" (*all things*, verb, prepositional phrases). There is also the less than perfect chiastic parallel between 1:17a and 1:17b: "And he is before all things" (personal pronoun, verb, *all things*) and "and all things in him hold together" (*all things*, personal pronoun, verb).

Finally, I refer my readers to the experience of everyone who wants to read serious poetry. You need to dust off your dictionary, for you must finger-walk incessantly through its pages as you try to figure out the uncommon vocabulary of serious poetry. I give a few examples of how this experience applies to Colossians 1:15-20. The adjective "visible" (Greek: *horatos*) in 1:16c, the verb "to be preeminent" (Greek: *proteuein*) in 1:18c, the verb "to make peace" (Greek: *eirenopoiein*) in 1:20b, and the phrase "the blood of his cross" (Greek: *haima tou staurou autou*) in 1:20b are found nowhere else in the New Testament. Also, the only occurrence in the Pauline letters of the noun "thrones" (Greek: *thronoi*) is found in 1:16d.

Why such a density of uncommon words in six verses? My answer is twofold. We are dealing with poetry. Also, we are pondering traditional material, formulated in a vocabulary different from that ordinarily used by the author. For those who doubt the veracity of my second answer, I refer them to a common experience. As you read through a term paper you gain a fairly good grasp of the author's vocabulary and style. Then at a certain point in the paper you come across pages written in a different, perhaps more elegant and clear style. Then you return again to the regular style of the author of the term paper. It took me one reading of term papers to detect this type of borrowing. In a similar sense, the author of Colossians flattered the composer of the hymn found in 1:15-20 by quoting it in its entirety with its uncommon vocabulary, at the beginning of his letter.

By means of special vocabulary, parallelisms within and between the two stanzas, artistic repetition of prepositions, and the refrain "all things," the composer of Colossians 1:15-20 has created a wondrous hymn to draw attention to the one who is absolute in every way—Jesus Christ.

Perhaps we can tune into the composer's artistic wavelength by reflecting upon another two-stanza religious poem, whose deepest focus is Christ the Lord. I refer to the sonnet, "The Windhover: To Christ our Lord," by the Jesuit Gerard Manley Hopkins, who was born in England in 1844 and died in Ireland in 1889. In struggling to understand Hopkins' sonnet, we will find ourselves soaring within our religious imaginations under the power of language fashioned by an expert wordsmith, and we'll find numerous interpretive challenges analogous to those we'll face in Colossians 1:15-20.

The Windhover: To Christ our Lord

I caught this morning morning's minion, kingdom of daylight's
  dauphin, dapple-dawn-drawn Falcon, in his riding
Of the rolling level underneath him steady air, and striding
High there, how he rung upon the rein of a wimpling wing
In his ecstasy! then off, off forth on swing,
    As a skate's heel sweeps smooth on a bow-bend: the hurl and
      gliding
Rebuffed the big wind. My heart in hiding
Stirred for a bird,—the achieve of, the mastery of the thing!

Brute beauty and valour and act, oh, air, pride, plume, here
    Buckle! AND the fire that breaks from thee, then, a billion
Times told lovelier, more dangerous, O my chevalier!

  No wonder of it: sheer plod makes plough down sillion
Shine, and blue-bleak embers, ah my dear,
    Fall, gall themselves, and gash gold-vermilion.

My comments on this marvelous poem will be brief and will
parallel what I have said above about the poem in Colossians.
First, both Colossians 1:15-20 and "The Windhover" have two
stanzas. In its sonnet form the first stanza of "The Windhover"
has eight lines while its second stanza has six lines. Second, with
regard to content, the first stanza of "The Windhover" largely focuses on the achievements of the material creature, the falcon,
whereas its second stanza accentuates the deeper, spiritual,
Christ-like meaning of the falcon's accomplishments. Recall the
scholarly opinion about the two stanzas of Colossians 1:15-20:
the first stanza deals with creation while the second stanza focuses on re-creation. Yet just as there is tension between the
goodness of all creation in the first stanza and the need for all
creation to be reconciled in the second stanza, so too is there tension between the two stanzas of "The Windhover." While there
is admiration for the falcon in stanza one, there is apprehension
about the pain inherent in getting involved with the "lovelier,
more dangerous" fire of Jesus Christ and being the subject or object of "fall, gall, and gash."

Third, there is rhythm and rhyme galore in "The Windhover."
Take, for example, "riding," "striding," "gliding," and "hiding" in

the first stanza. And "here," "chevalier," and "dear" in the second stanza paralleled by "billion," "sillion," and "vermilion."

Fourth, there is strange vocabulary. Hopkins has taken three terms from the world of knighthood: "minion" (servile follower); "dauphin" (crown prince); "chevalier" (knight). And I would wager that "dapple" (marked with spots) is not part of your common vocabulary. And would you believe it? Although we have millions of words in the English language, Hopkins coined a new one in "sillion," which probably means "furrow." Needless to say, "sillion" doesn't bear the theological weight of the verb "making peace" in Colossians 1:20b, but it has this in common with it: both are very rare or even neologisms (technically and in Greek: *hapax legomena*).

Fifth, I build upon my previous point by highlighting vocabulary which is key to the meaning of "The Windhover," but which is patient of multiple meanings. I refer to line ten: "Buckle! AND." Hopkins wrote the exclamation point and put the word "and" in capitals. Is "buckle" an imperative? Does "buckle" refer to "buckle up" your seat belts or the walls and floor "buckled under" the heat of the fire or some other meaning of "buckle"? And then what about "AND"? I prefer the meaning of the buckling which opens up solid materials and reveals the fire deep within. For me, the second stanza reveals the falcon as Christ, "my chevalier," whose fire of life is far more lovely and dangerous than that of any grand predator bird performing according to its nature. Again the parallels between important and multilayered vocabulary in "The Windhover" and Colossians 1:15-20 are telling. The Arian controversy revolved around the meaning of Colossians 1:15b: "the firstborn of all creation." That is, did this mean that Jesus Christ is the supreme creature or the one who is before all creation? What does "the fullness" in 1:19 mean? All the heavenly aeons, as in Gnosticism? Or all God's power for goodness? Finally, are the terms "principalities and powers" used in the same meaning in 1:16e, 2:10, and 2:15? Happily, linguistic and theological investigations have settled the issue of the meaning of 1:15b, "the firstborn of all creation," and of 1:19, "the fullness." In our third section on key concepts and images we will return to the unsettled issue of the meaning of "principalities and powers."

I conclude this section by referring to the deep Christology which underlies Hopkins' poem, a Christology based on the interpretation of Colossians 1:15-18 championed by the Franciscan theologian, Blessed John Duns Scotus (ca. 1265–1308). As Elizabeth Jennings observes: "Duns Scotus was an important influence since his theology included the belief that God the Son would have become man even if Adam had not fallen from grace. This unusual attitude towards the Incarnation, not shared, for example, by Aquinas, had a powerful effect on Hopkins' poetry in that it enabled him to see the Incarnation as more than simply the means of man's redemption. For him, such a doctrine glorified the material world and was, perhaps, largely responsible for the lovely, carefree poems of praise such as . . . 'The Windhover' . . . " (1975, 195). Jennings' point about the influence of Duns Scotus' Christology on Hopkins' poetry is perhaps best seen in the final lines of his sonnet, "As kingfishers catch fire":

> Christ—for Christ plays in ten thousand places,
> Lovely in limbs, and lovely in eyes not his
> To the Father through the features of men's faces.

In the final section of this chapter I will return to the question of the relevance of Duns Scotus' interpretation of Colossians 1:15-20 for today's ecological concerns.

B. THE CONTEXT

Before treating the immediate and broader context of Colossians 1:15-20, I want to make explicit what has been implicit in my discussions so far. That is, in my opinion the author of Colossians was not Paul, but a trusted Pauline disciple writing in the 60s to a church which Paul did not found, but which was perceived as needing further instruction in faith because of the threats posed by some opponents. I will provide more information about these opponents in the section below on broader context.

Also, I want to remind my readers of the cultural context within which Colossians was written and which I've called "an age of anxiety" in my previous chapter on backgrounds. In his excellent commentary on Colossians, Eduard Schweizer gives the following description of the Hellenistic world at the time of the writing of Colossians: "The stability of the world has become problematic. The struggle of the elements of nature (water, air, earth, and fire) against one another expresses itself in catastrophes and threatens to lead to a complete breakdown of the universe. The fragile nature of the world and its order is experienced everywhere, and the individual seems like a prisoner of nature, a nature at war with itself" (1982, 80). In all fairness to this cultural context, however, I must observe, along with Richard E. DeMaris (1994, 94–96), that Schweizer may have painted too pessimistic a picture. There were some philosophers and divines who sometimes detected order or reason or *logos* in the way the elements of nature normally operate. Incidentally, "elements of nature/universe" is a translation of the Greek phrase which occurs in Colossians 2:8 and 2:20. In Greek the phrase is *stoicheia tou kosmou*. The NAB translation is "elemental powers of the world."

Commentators have noted that the *immediate context* of Colossians 1:14 and 1:22 underlines the truth that it is through Christ and his cross that believers have "forgiveness of sins" and are "reconciled." Thus, by means of the brackets of 1:14 and 1:22 the author endeavors to eliminate any possible interpretation that the reconciliation sung about in 1:20a was merely cosmic, automatic, and did not require Christ's salvific action or any moral response from believers.

Further, the immediate context of 2:2-3 makes clear on what grounds the author of Colossians will face the "philosophers" who threaten the community's faith. The author knows and understands the "mystery of God, Christ, in whom are hidden all the treasures of wisdom and knowledge." Implied is that these errorists lack such knowledge and understanding. The author makes this claim explicit in 2:8: the errorists proclaim a philosophy "according to human tradition, according to the elemental powers of the world, and not according to Christ."

In dealing with the *broader context* for 1:15-20, I will give special attention to 2:4–3:12. I begin with 2:8, 16-23, which Richard DeMaris has termed "the polemical core in Colossians." Granted all the methodological hazards of trying to reconstruct the viewpoint(s) of the "errorists" from the author's attack on their tenets,

DeMaris quite plausibly maintains that the major issue between the author and the "errorists" involved the pursuit and acquisition of divine knowledge. The "philosophers" at Colossae pursued their wisdom in multiple ways. First, they relied on the "elemental powers of the universe," whose harmony and proportion reflected a divine ordering. And since Jesus Christ had established peace among all things (all elements) once and for all (see 1:20b), they had assurance that ordering and balance among the elements were secured. Second, through ascetical practices of fasting, abstinence, and observance of special days they tried to liberate their minds from distractions and prepare themselves to receive and comprehend revelatory insight from above. Third, like thousands of their compatriots they reverenced demons/angels, who acted as messengers between heaven and earth (DeMaris 1994, 131–32, 142).

In 2:8, 16-23, the author vigorously argues that the three avenues just described do not lead one to divine knowledge. Repeating in different ways his foundational point that only in Christ is there wisdom (2:3), the author maintains that dying with Christ in baptism liberated the Colossians from (the study or control of) the elemental powers of the universe (2:20). That is, no divine knowledge will come from study of what we today would call first principles, natural law, and the elements by which all reality is held together. Further, fastings and such may well have an effect contrary to the ecstatic experience anticipated, for they may set into motion drives to gratify the flesh (2:23). Moreover, seeking revelation from angels and engaging in profound investigations of visionary experiences will not lead to humility, but to pride and community-destroying elitism (2:18). In brief, the author insists that the Colossians stick close to Christ, the head (2:19), that is, they must adhere to the wisdom of the hymn and not wander down avenues which might be heralded as passages to divine wisdom, but which in reality are dead ends.

It seems that the goal of the author's polemic against the errorists is to prompt his readers to hasten back to the wisdom of Colossians 1:15-20 and abandon any inkling they might have had to find divine knowledge in any other place than in Christ. But the author does not want his readers to hasten back too fast to the traditional material of 1:15-10. First, they must learn how he has interpreted it by the teaching of 2:9-15, which he has inserted right into the middle of the polemical core of 2:8, 16-23. To 2:9-15 I now turn.

For our purposes I limit our discussion of 2:9-15 to what the author says about Christ and the principalities and powers in 2:10 and 2:15. Recall that the principalities and powers were positively mentioned in 1:16e of the hymn as having been created in Jesus Christ and in 1:20a as having been reconciled. 2:9 says that Christ is head, that is, lord, of every principality and power. That's about the same thing the hymn itself implied, although when the specific word "head" is mentioned in 1:18a, reference is made to the body, the Church. So far, so good. In 2:15, however, the author goes beyond what the hymn said in 1:20a and 1:20b about "reconciliation" and "peacemaking" and says that through his cross Christ has despoiled the principalities and powers. This imagery is derived from the Roman triumphal procession, the highest honor Rome could bestow on its conquering heroes, and graphically shows how God has publicly shamed the principalities and powers and exposed them in his triumphal procession through Christ's cross. With studied understatement Wayne A. Meeks observes that the metaphor of triumph over the cosmic powers "betrays a rather more negative evaluation of them than does the reconciliation metaphor of the hymn" (1979, 211). Why this negative evaluation of the principalities and powers? Perhaps they are conceived as the divine powers which "stand behind the elements and move them" (Schweizer 1982, 81). And since the author has such a low regard of these elements, he paints the principalities and powers in the same negative light. Would that the author had been more clear about what the errorists said about the relationship between the elemental powers of the universe and the principalities and powers! In any case, we know that the author viewed both negatively, whereas the hymn of 1:15-20 had a more positive regard for the principalities and powers.

Finally, I call to your attention briefly the significance of 3:11 in the broader context of 1:15-20. Meeks makes the excellent point that the hymn of 1:15-20 praises Jesus Christ as the one who restores a created but lost unity. And if we look at the unification formula in 3:11, we begin to glimpse that baptism was a ritual actualization among humankind of that universal and cosmic restoration to unity. 3:11 reads: "Here there is not Greek and Jew, circumcision, and uncircumcision, barbarian, Scythian, slave, free; but Christ is all and in all." Thus, in the Church and through baptism exist all stripes of humanity, whose restoration and reconciliation have been effected through Jesus Christ. Put another way, when we read 1:18a, "and Jesus Christ is the head of the body, the church," we are made aware of the profound truth that the One who holds all things together (1:17b) has also put them back together again—in the Church. In terms of content and style 1:18a not only concludes the first stanza of the hymn about creation, but it also leads into the second stanza about restoration and reconciliation.

After this extensive discussion of the context of Colossians 1:15-20, I need to review where we've been and what we've seen. It seems clear that the author of Colossians and the philosophers belonged to the people of their time who were searching for a deeper meaning in life, who were investigating the teachings and practices of various philosophies and religions to achieve unity between themselves and God, between themselves and peoples of other nations, and between themselves and nature/the cosmos. Both the author of Colossians and the philosophers accepted the truth of the hymn of Colossians 1:15-20, but they differed in how this hymn was to be interpreted.

The philosophers had a high regard for the knowledge to be derived from the study of the elemental principles of the universe whereas the author of Colossians degrades such knowledge, preferring exclusively the wisdom of Jesus Christ. The author of Colossians viewed the principalities and powers as bringers of evil, who had to be despoiled and humbled by the death of Jesus Christ on the cross. It would seem that the philosophers had a higher regard for these powerful creatures.

Having shown how the immediate and broader contexts of the hymn of Colossians 1:15-20 have aided its interpretation, I want to turn next to its key concepts and images. We may well find that the hymn used concepts and images which were open to the various interpretations we have found in the polemical core of Colossians 2:8, 16-23, and in the author's theology and Christology of 2:9-15.

C. KEY CONCEPTS AND IMAGES

I want to consider four key concepts and images, all of which are interrelated: (1) the Old Testament background of Colossians 1:15-20; (2) the absolute primacy of Jesus Christ; (3) the principalities and powers; and (4) reconciliation and peacemaking.

In talking about *the Old Testament background* of Colossians 1:15-20, I do not mean to say that there are not some Gnostic and philosophical parallels which provide helpful interpretive background to our hymn. Such do exist. For example, recall the philosophical background I noted earlier about the prepositions in, for, and through. I also recall the fleeting reference I made earlier to a possible Gnostic background for understanding "fullness" (Greek: *pleroma*) in 1:19. In stressing the Old Testament background, I advise my readers that it provides the most explanatory parallels. Pragmatically stated, the Old Testament background, especially that of the wisdom literature, gives me the most interpretation for my exegetical dollar.

There is considerable truth in the claim which N. T. Wright makes that the wisdom literature is not the total answer to the background for Colossians 1:15-20. Rather, both stanzas of this hymn should be interpreted from the Jewish worldview, of which the wisdom literature is merely one facet. That is, the Old Testament assumes that the redeeming/electing God is also the creator God and vice versa. In Wright's own words: "For this worldview, there is one God; he made the world, and is neither identified with it (as in pantheism and its various pagan cousins) nor detached from it (as in dualism); he is in covenant with Israel; and he will, in fulfilling that covenant, reclaim and redeem his whole creation from that which at present corrupts and threatens it" (1990, 453).

Granted the overall merit of Wright's observations, I still think it helpful to rehearse the wisdom background of Colossians 1:15-20, bearing in mind that these wisdom parallels only help explicate the hymn's first stanza. That is, we'll have to find a different background for the second stanza. I follow Mary Rose D'Angelo's list of parallels between wisdom (in Greek: the feminine noun *sophia*) and Colossians 1:15-20 (1994, 318):

Colossians 1:15a:	"the image of the invisible God"
Wisdom 7:26:	"[Wisdom] is the refulgence of eternal light, the spotless mirror of God, the image of God's goodness."
Colossians 1:15b:	"the firstborn of all creation"
Proverbs 8:22:	"The Lord begot me [Wisdom], the firstborn of his ways, the forerunner of his prodigies of long ago."
Sirach 24:9:	"Before all ages, in the beginning, he created me [Wisdom], and through the ages I shall not cease to be."
Colossians 1:16ab:	"For in him were created all things in heaven and on earth"
Wisdom 7:22:	"For Wisdom, the artificer of all, taught me."
Proverbs 3:19-20:	"The Lord by wisdom founded the earth, established the heavens by understanding; by his knowledge the depths break open, and the clouds drop dew."
Proverbs 8:23, 30:	"From of old I [Wisdom] was poured forth, at the first, before the earth. . . . Then [at creation] was I beside God as God's master worker, and I was God's delight day by day, playing before God all the while."

By means of Jewish wisdom theology the composer of Colossians 1:15-20 created one of Christianity's first and loftiest Christologies. As commentators continually remind us, this hymn is being sung in praise of someone who was executed as a criminal in a remote part of the Roman Empire some thirty years earlier. Yet this hymn mentions the human life of Jesus Christ only once, and that by means of the theologically freighted expression, "blood of his cross" (1:20b). This is not the narrative Christology of the four gospels, although John's Gospel, especially through its hymnic prologue about God's Logos, provides some parallels to the Christology of Colossians 1:15-20. We are viewing protology at work, as the composer takes us behind the scenes, before creation occurred, and struggles to express that in Jesus Christ God has manifested God's wisdom and plan for all of creation. Just as wisdom represents God to the outside, that is, as God's image, so too does Jesus Christ, as God's image. And Jesus Christ has manifested that wisdom not just at the beginning of his earthly life, not just through his death and resurrection, but indeed from the very beginning (see 1:18b).

Let me put the wisdom Christology of the Colossians in other terms. God is not so transcendent that God is not immanent to creation. That immanence might be seen through the eyes of Genesis 1:26: God created human beings in God's image. That immanence might be seen in the wisdom of God, the image of God. But now the composer of 1:15-20 says: God has become immanent in Jesus Christ, God's all-encompassing and perfect image. Or as N. T. Wright expresses this mystery: "The pre-existent lord of the world has become the human lord of the world, and in so doing has reflected fully, for the eyes of the world to see, the God whose human image he has now come to bear. This explains, among other things, the nature of the language often used to describe him: as in 2 Cor 8.9, the pre-existent one, who (strictly speaking) had not yet 'become' Jesus of Nazareth, can be referred to by that name in advance, much as we might say 'the Queen was born in 1925'" (1990, 461). If I replace "Queen" with "President," citizens of the United States might more readily appreciate the force of Wright's analogy: How can one say that the President was born in 1925 when she didn't become President until her inauguration in 1996?

My second key concept—*the absolute primacy of Jesus Christ*—builds upon the point just mentioned regarding the lordship of Jesus Christ. Perhaps "the absolute primacy of Jesus Christ" is unfamiliar terminology to some of my readers, for it comes from a centuries-old Roman Catholic tradition, brought to full articulation by the Franciscan medieval theologian John Duns Scotus, and insists on the absolute priority of God's will and grace and on the secondary role of human sin. Put another way, even if women and men had not sinned, God would still have expressed his love for humanity through the self-communication of the Incarnation. I turn, however, to a Jesuit New Testament scholar rather than a Franciscan one, to find words to express what Colossians 1:15-20 says about Jesus Christ's primacy.

Jean-Noël Aletti, S.J., has detailed six ways in which Colossians 1:15-20 expresses the primacy of Christ (1981, 93–94). It should be noted that each one of the six ways finds expression in both stanzas of the hymn and lends weight to Aletti's argument that the composer is a consummate artist and theologian. The first way is that of *eminence*. In the first stanza eminence is found in the expressions "firstborn" (1:15b) and "image" (1:15a). In the second stanza 1:18c gives voice to this notion: "he himself might be *preeminent.*"

The second way is that of *universality*. I would refer my readers to my translation of 1:15-20 at the beginning of this chapter where I italicized the eight references to "all things." Here I merely mention the references given by Aletti. In stanza one we have: "all creation" (1:15b); "all things" (1:16a, f, 17b); "before all things" (1:17a plus the list in 1:16b-e). In the second stanza we find: "all things" in 1:20a and "whether those on earth or those in heaven" in 1:20c.

The third way is that of *uniqueness* or the insistence that it is solely and uniquely Jesus Christ who is and does what the hymn says. The easiest way to perceive this point is to review my translation of 1:15-20 at the beginning of this chapter where I have highlighted the prepositional phrases with boldfaced print. In stanza one you will see "in him" in 1:16a, and "through him" and "for him" in 1:16f, and "in him" in 1:17b. In the second stanza there is "he himself" in 1:18c, "in him" in 1:19, "through him" and "for him" in 1:20a and "through him" in 1:20b. For those who know Greek I call your attention to the fact that 1:17a and 1:18a use *autos* to make it explicit that it is Christ only who is the subject of the verb that follows.

Aletti's fourth way is a little subtle and is a variation of the second way of universality. The fourth way of primacy is that of *totality* (on all levels). In the first stanza this way finds expression on the level of creation: "were created" (1:16a, f). Also on the level of modality this way is found in the prepositions: "in" (1:16a and 1:17b); "through" (1:16f); "for" (1:16f). Moreover, the level of "being held together" or "being sustained in existence" (1:17b) is part of the fourth way. In the second stanza "in all things" shows Christ's primacy on every level of being. And finally 1:20a is rich as it sings of the reconciliation of all through Christ and for Christ.

The fifth way is that of *priority*. "Firstborn" (1:15b) and "before all things" are the means by which the first stanza sings of Christ's primacy in this regard. In the second stanza "the beginning" and "firstborn of the dead" (1:18b) proclaim loudly this aspect of Christ's primacy.

The final way is that of *definitive accomplishment.* What is said of Christ in the two stanzas of the hymn is not the language of a commencement, but that of a jubilee celebration. That is, we do not sing congratulations about the future accomplishments of one embarking on a new career, but of things already accomplished by an individual, in this instance, Christ. Thus, Christ is already "the image of the invisible God" (1:15a) and "the firstborn of all creation" (1:15b). Christ is already "the beginning" and "the firstborn from the dead" (1:18b). Christ is already "the head of the body, the church" (1:18a). Christ is already the one in whom reconciliation and peace were accomplished (1:20a, b). Again note how these definitive accomplishments link together the two stanzas which make up our hymn.

Perhaps, other Christian traditions have another way of articulating what Aletti and theologians centuries before him have termed the primacy of Christ in 1:15-20. In classroom discussions of my book these might surface. For the present I summarize my second key concept and image. In Christ and through Christ are eminence, universality, uniqueness, totality, priority, and definitive accomplishments. That is, Colossians 1:15-20 celebrates in song the absolute primacy of Jesus Christ.

In our discussion earlier in this chapter of the broader context of Colossians 1:15-20 I remarked that the author of Colossians seems to have a view of *principalities and powers* different from that of the composer of the hymn. In 2:15 the author states that through his cross Christ has despoiled the principalities and powers. This statement seems to stand in explicit contradiction to 1:16e which states that the same principalities and powers are good. On a certain level we might be tempted to dismiss this seeming contradiction as something contrived by scholars to keep them in the business of interpretation. But on a very serious level we are coming face to face with the problem of who is actually in control of our lives. We ourselves? We with Jesus Christ? We as driven hither and yon by fate? We as controlled by institutional power run amok? I will open a perspective on this very large and very real contemporary issue by using the insights of Walter Wink in his book *Naming the Powers* (1984).

Perhaps Wink's major contribution is to have investigated all the New Testament texts which talk about principalities and powers (Greek: *archai kai exousiai*) and related terms and not to have limited himself to texts from the Pauline letters. Two key Gospel passages are Luke 12:11 and 20:20. I adapt the NAB translation of Luke 12:11: "When they take you before synagogues and before principalities and powers *(archai kai exousiai),* do not worry about how or what your defense will be or about what you are to say." Surely, by principalities and powers Jesus is not referring to good or bad angels. In Luke 20:20 the singular of principalities and powers is used and in clear reference to a human being in a governmental position of authority. Again I modify the NAB: "They watched Jesus closely and sent agents pretending to be righteous who were to trap him in speech, in order to hand him over to the principality and power of the governor."

I think that it is justifiable to quote an entire paragraph from Wink's study in order to capture some of the revolutionary force of his analysis:

> These Powers are both heavenly and earthly, divine and human, spiritual and political, invisible and structural. The clearest statement of this is Col. 1:16, which should have been made the standard for all discussions of the Powers: "For in him [the Son] all things were created, in heaven and on earth, visible and invisible, whether thrones *(thronoi)* or dominions *(kyriotetes)* or principalities *(archai)* or authorities *(exousiai)*—all things were created through him and for him." The parallelism of the Greek, ably rendered here by the RSV, indicates that these Powers are themselves both earthly *and* heavenly, visible *and* invisible. We would expect them to include human agents, social structures and systems, and also divine powers. The reiteration of "whether on earth or in heaven" in v. 20 connects back to v. 16 and suggests that the cosmic reconciliation which God is bringing about through Christ will specifically include these powers, human and divine, and that no reconciliation would be complete without them (1984, 11).

What direct bearing does Wink's study have on the meaning of Colossians 1:16c-e? We should not put the "powers" in a negative light as the author of Colossians seems to have done in 2:15. If we follow the interpretation of the author of Colossians, we may miss the first century and contemporary meaning(s) of 1:16c-e. In my "Reflection Starters," I will return to this point as I look, through Wink's eyes and those of the composer of Colossians 1:15-20, at the good and the evil of government and other institutions.

My final key concept and image accentuates 1:20a and 1:20b and deals with *reconciliation and making peace.* From what I have said so far in this chapter, it is obvious that there is a tension between the *good* creation of the first stanza and the need for *bad* creation to be reconciled in the second stanza. The composer of the hymn does not tell us what went awry and necessitated that creation be re-created. While that is true, it will be helpful to seek for some background material which will help us interpret 1:20ab.

That background is not found in Israel's Wisdom literature, but in the philosophical-religious speculation of Philo of Alexandria, a contemporary of St. Paul, who used philosophical categories to make sense of his Jewish religious belief, first for himself and then for his fellow Jewish believers and interested non-Jews. Philo's works give us some indication of the human quest for peace. In Philo's *Special Laws,* 192 the word "peacemaker" occurs, but is nowhere else in Philo's voluminous writings. And this term is found in a context in which Philo describes the trumpet of the Jewish New Year festival as the signal for the end of war, "a cessation which God as founder and protector of peace, inaugurates; peace, that is, between the parts of the universe that are fighting against each other within the world of nature" (Schweizer 1982, 80). This parallel from Philo does not mean that Christ's death on the cross is the beginning of a New Year of peace. Rather, Philo's parallel gives evidence, in Jewish symbols, of the universal human and religious longing for peace, not just between humans but also between warring parties in the universe, be these fire, water, air, or earth in the form of brush fires, floods, cyclones, or earthquakes.

What Philo expressed in the Jewish symbol of New Year the composer of Colossians 1:20ab expresses through a fundamental

Christian symbol, the Cross. That is, 1:20ab sings that the peace and reconciliation, universally longed for, has been achieved through Jesus Christ and his death on the cross. Earth and heaven are united. What was lost is restored. But such unification and such restoration are not automatic. They have a price: the shedding of Christ's blood on the cross. And as Wayne Meeks has reminded us, Christians must pay the price of baptismal commitment. For the cosmic drama of reconciliation is reenacted ritually in baptism where women and men must divest themselves of political, social, and ethnic ideologies and become one in the Church (see 3:11).

As we come to the conclusion of this section on key concepts and images, we might well ask what our four points have contributed to our comprehension of the Christologically rich hymn of Colossians 1:15-20. Christ, who lived, taught, and was crucified in an obscure part of the Roman Empire, was with God at the beginning of all things. He holds all things together. And as the firstborn from the dead, he is the conqueror of that power which holds all things in thralldom, death. Christ has primacy in everything and in every way. Through Christ and for Christ God has fulfilled the longings of the human heart for peace and a cessation of cosmic and human warfare.

D. REFLECTION STARTERS

Although I have sprinkled reflections throughout the previous three sections of this chapter, now is the time to give special attention to four reflections.

I begin with a reflection about one aspect of the Christology of Colossians 1:15-20 and do so by quoting an insight of Amos N. Wilder: "Primitive Christian poetry is spoken, as it were, at the beginning of a world, indeed, at the beginning of the world. Its substance and forms are eloquent, then, of this hour, an hour, indeed, which ever renews itself for faith" (1971, 116). Yes, 1:15-20 invites us, challenges us to take flight in our religious imaginations back to the beginning, nay, before the beginning and to see Christ thoroughly enjoying creating and longing to become human to express tangibly God's unconditional love for all human and nonhuman creation.

A second reflection takes the following shape. During this era of ecological concern Colossians 1:15-20 reminds us of the solemn truths that creation is good and that reconciliation is for all. When Christians sing 1:15-20, as they do, for example, on Wednesdays at vespers, they are celebrating God's creative concern for all. Or as Eduard Schweizer phrases this truth: "They will therefore bring again and again before God everyone and everything, believers and nonbelievers, human and nonhuman creation, and demand his love for them" (1982, 300). Implied in the statement, "demand his love for them," is the fact that Christians themselves will display in their lives God's love for everyone and everything, believers and nonbelievers, human and nonhuman creation. Thus, reconciliation is not just for my part of the universe while I exploit other parts, thereby creating ecological chaos. Put another way, singing 1:15-20 in church is one thing. Living out its profound message in daily life is another. As the religious aphorism has it: You only know as much as you do.

Creation is not only good. It is Christic, for it bears the imprint of the one in whose image it was created—Christ. Perhaps it is easiest to try to see Christ in one's fellow human beings, be they rich or homeless, and to treat them reverently as Dorothy Day of the Catholic Worker did for decades. But how does one even begin to see Christ in nonhuman creatures? Earlier we saw how Gerard Manley Hopkins was able to see Christ the Lord behind and through the actions of a falcon in his poem, "The Windhover." I now suggest that St. Francis of Assisi provides many components of an answer in his "Canticle of Brother Sun," wherein he calls the elements of the universe "brother" and "sister." With such human terms of endearment Francis, perhaps too mystical for some, bridges the gap between human and inhuman, animate and inanimate and says volumes for today's world as the Patron of Ecologists, proclaimed such by Pope John Paul II in 1979. As I quote from Francis' canticle, I remind my readers that Sir William Walton has set this canticle to music under the title "Cantico del Sole" (available on CD from Chandos no. 9222).

The Canticle of Brother Sun

Most high, all-powerful, all good, Lord!
　All praise is yours, all glory, all honor
　And all blessing.
To you, alone, Most High, do they belong.
　No mortal lips are worthy
　To pronounce your name.
All praise be yours, my Lord, through all that you have made,
　And first my lord Brother Sun,
　Who brings the day; and light you give to us through him.
How beautiful is he, how radiant in all his splendor!
　Of you, Most High, he bears the likeness.
All praise be yours, my Lord, through Sister Moon and Stars;
　In the heavens you have made them, bright
　And precious and fair.
All praise be yours, my Lord, through Brothers Wind and Air,
　And fair and stormy, all the weather's moods,
　By which you cherish all that you have made.
All praise be yours, my Lord, through Sister Water,
　So useful, lowly, precious and pure.
All praise be yours, my Lord, through Brother Fire,
　Through whom you brighten up the night.
　How beautiful is he, how joyful! Full of power and strength.
All praise be yours, my Lord, through Sister Earth, our mother,
　Who feeds us in her sovereignty and produces
　Various fruits with colored flowers and herbs.
All praise be yours, my Lord, through those who grant pardon
　For love of you; through those who endure
　Sickness and trial.
Happy those who endure in peace,
　By you, Most High, they will be crowned.
All praise be yours, my Lord, through Sister Death,
　From whose embrace no mortal can escape.
Woe to those who die in mortal sin!
　Happy those She finds doing your will!
　The second death can do no harm to them.
Praise and bless my Lord, and give him thanks,
　And serve him with great humility (Habig 1973, 130–31).

It should be noted that Francis' canticle, like Colossians 1:15-20, sings of creation and re-creation. For the latter term, Francis uses "pardon" and "peace." Further, Francis does not fear the potential chaos of the elements of the universe in earthquake, hurricane, forest fire, and flash flood. Rather he honors and praises the elements for all the good they are and do. They are brother and sister.

The focus of my third reflection is on a feminist critique of Colossians. The author of Colossians, who in Colossians 2 took issue with some tenets of the philosophers, might not be surprised that contemporary scholars are taking issue with some of his tenets and the way he may have been led in the controversy reflected in Colossians 2 to have stated things too narrowly. Let me be more specific.

In her commentary on Colossians, Mary Rose D'Angelo is highly critical of the author's use of the household codes in 3:18–4:1 wherein wives are instructed to be subordinate to their husbands and slaves are directed to obey their human masters in everything. In her feminist critique of 3:18–4:1, D'Angelo not only finds fault with the household codes themselves, but also and especially with their theological underpinning: "Despite its brevity and simplicity, Colossians' code is not merely conventional exhortation but the integral consequence of Christ's universal lordship. If that universal lordship liberates from the heavenly powers and authorities, it nevertheless affirms the patriarchal rule of the masters of this world" (1994, 322).

While D'Angelo may be right that the author of Colossians "affirms the patriarchal rule of the masters of this world," she has overstated her case that "Colossians' code is . . . the integral consequence of Christ's universal lordship." How one author, even be he the author of the canonical Colossians, views Christ's universal lordship does not determine that this view is the only one or "the integral consequence of Christ's universal lordship." As I have stated frequently in my section above on the broader context of 1:15-20, the author of Colossians has a view of the principalities and powers and even of the elements of the universe which is different from that of the hymn itself. Expressed differently, in the canonical Colossians there are two views of the meaning of Christ's universal lordship: that of the author of Colossians and that of 1:15-20. In interpreting 1:15-20 as Walter Wink has done (see reflection four following), we may find a way, from within Colossians itself, to attend to D'Angelo's critique.

While we await the insights of Wink in reflection four, I mention that Meeks calls our attention to the apologetic nature of the household codes, which answered the "common Roman complaint that foreign cults disrupted households and thus eventually the public order" (1979, 220, no. 33). In Colossians the household code "assures that the basic structure of the Christian household will resemble that which is insisted upon by society at large." If Meeks is correct, and I believe that he is, then we have one way of answering D'Angelo's critique. That is, let's give shape to a basic structure of Christian household today which will resemble that which society today enjoins upon its people. Of course, giving shape to such a basic structure is not an easy endeavor. Nor is it facile to ascertain the household structure which society today requires of its people. But the components are at hand to prevent the present and future generations from reading Colossians 3:18-4:1 as eternal and unalterable law. In brief, D'Angelo has alerted our attention to the fact that Scripture is not a museum piece nor something to be mouthed at the Church's liturgy, but lays awesome responsibilities upon preachers and teachers who must help believers to assimilate its demanding meanings for daily life.

Walter Wink's trilogy on the "powers" leads us into my fourth reflection on the social justice implications of Colossians 1:15-20. For the powers are not just spiritual powers, but can also be today's institutions, systems, and structures which have a compelling force for good or evil which goes beyond any one individual or individual manifestation of the force. Take as one example the institution of "the old boys' club," which can and has taken on a life of its own to exclude women and other people of lesser station in life. In order to try on Walter Wink's thought processes about the social justice implications of the powers, I want to repeat part of an earlier quotation. In talking about 1:16, Wink writes: "We would expect them (the Powers) to include human agents, social structures and systems, and also divine powers" (1984, 11). Wink goes on to say that reconciliation through Christ is also for the sake of these powers (see 1:20). Put another way, according to the theology of the composer of the hymn the powers are good, have fallen, and are in need of reconciliation. As we have seen time and time again, that is not necessarily the total view of the author of Colossians in 2:9, 15. So far, so good.

Wink's next step is to take with utmost seriousness the wisdom background of 1:15-20, especially as it applies to 1:20b: "through the blood of his cross." Wisdom personified in Christ has been crucified. Again, so far, so good.

Wink's final step consists in interpreting 1:15-20, especially 1:20b by means of the Pauline statement in 1 Corinthians 2:6-8: "Yet we do speak a wisdom to those who are mature, but not a wisdom of this age, nor of the rulers of this age who are passing away. Rather we speak God's wisdom, mysterious, hidden, which God predetermined before the ages for our glory, and which none of the rulers of this age knew for, if they had known it, they would not have crucified the Lord of glory." Without entering into a lengthy interpretation of 1 Corinthians 2:6-8, we can make the following assumptions: (1) Christ is God's wisdom; (2) "rulers of this age" refer to both human and demonic powers (Wink 1984, 44–45). With the aforementioned notions in mind, we can begin tentative, but very serious reflection upon the powers and the implications of their reality for social justice in today's world.

At this point I refer back to D'Angelo's critique of the patriarchy of Colossians 3:18–4:1. Indeed, 1:16 sings that the powers are good and 1:20 sings that the powers have been reconciled through the blood of the Cross. But does that mean that in singing of such goodness and reconciliation, the worshiping community receives instantaneous communication about the nature of the powers that afflict them and about the necessary steps to take to neutralize them? At the time when Colossians was written, believers may have been primarily concerned with the powers of fate and magic, gained insight from the Christian community on how to neutralize them, and praised Christ for liberation from their clutches. Today socially enlightened Christians may name as powers for their fellow believers some of the ideologies inherent in the socialization processes by which we become men and women and relate to one another as such in our society. Such ideologies may truly be the powers today, for us.

I conclude my reflection upon the social justice dimension of Colossians 1:15-20 with a challenge to myself and to my readers: How do we name the powers in their goodness and in their need for reconciliation? How do we ritualize that the powers are good, but need reconciliation? Finally, how do we actualize our praying of 1:15-20, our song to Christ our Cosmic Peacemaker?

For my final remark on the vastly complicated, but immensely fruitful Christological hymn of Colossians, I want to quote from another writing by Walter Wink. Readers must aver the fact that in this quotation Wink is talking about good powers that need much reconciliation: ". . . I remember hearing of a Native American woman who rejected an offer of companionship on her lonely walk home in the dead of night: 'No, I won't be afraid. We have songs for this.' There is another story, as well, of a man being crucified, crying out an old Israelite hymn sung by his people under duress: 'My God, my God why hast thou forsaken me?' That hymn, sung to its close, ends in an affirmation of God's steadfast love. . . . The Jew, too, could say, 'we have songs for this.' We, too, even today—however evil the Powers may be, however resistant to change and violence they may be in their self-defense, however nimble and crafty they are in crushing opposition—we, too, thanks to the Colossians Christ-hymn, can say, 'We have songs for this'" (Wink 1990, 242–43).

Praise the Lord for the songster artist who composed Colossians 1:15-20!

ANNOTATED BIBLIOGRAPHY

Aletti, Jean-Nöel. *Colossiens 1,15-20: Genre et exégèse du texte; Fonction de la thèmatique sapientelle.* Analecta Biblical 91. Rome: Biblical Institute Press, 1981. Aletti argues for the integral, nonredacted nature of the hymn of Colossians 1:15-20 and for its wisdom background.

D'Angelo, Mary Rose. "Colossians." *Searching the Scriptures. Volume Two: A Feminist Commentary.* Ed. Elisabeth Schüssler Fiorenza, 313–24. New York: Crossroad, 1994. Presents a challenging feminist critique of the theology and ethics of Colossians.

DeMaris, Richard E. *The Colossian Controversy: Wisdom in Dispute at Colossae.* Journal for the Study of the New Testament Supplement Series 96. Sheffield, England: JSOT Press, 1994. Surveys previous scholarship on the opponents of Colossians and investigates the "polemical core" (Col 2:8, 16-23) of Colossians by utilizing philosophical and archaeological backgrounds.

Habig, Marion A., ed. *St. Francis of Assisi: Writings and Early Biographies, English Omnibus of the Sources for the Life of St. Francis.* Chicago: Franciscan Herald Press, 1973.

Jennings, Elizabeth. "The Unity of Incarnation." *Gerard Manley Hopkins: Poems.* Casebook Series. Ed. Margaret Bottrall. London: Macmillan Press, 1975.

Käsemann, Ernst. "A Primitive Christian Baptismal Liturgy," in a book of his collected essays, *Essays on New Testament Themes,* 149–68. Naperville: Allenson, 1964. With his characteristic brilliance Käsemann sharpened the focus on the meaning of Colossians 1:15-20. Few scholars today accept his view that a Gnostic myth lies behind Colossians 1:15-20.

Lohse, Eduard. *Colossians and Philemon: A Commentary on the Epistles to the Colossians and to Philemon.* Hermeneia Commentary Series. Philadelphia: Fortress, 1971. Rich in background materials from various sources.

Martin, Ralph P. *Colossians and Philemon.* New Century Bible Commentary. Grand Rapids: Eerdmans, 1973. His interpretive thrust is captured in his comment on Colossians 1:20b: "This is his (Paul's) counterblow to gnostic redemption and reconciliation which works by non-moral fiat and automatic process" (p. 61).

Meeks, Wayne A. "In One Body: The Unity of Humankind in Colossians and Ephesians." *God's Christ and His People: Studies in Honour of Nils Alstrup Dahl.* Eds. Jacob Jervell and Wayne A. Meeks, 209–21. Oslo, Norway: Universitetsforlaget, 1979. Meeks offers this fertile insight: "That baptism dramatized a cosmic, not merely a human, restoration of unity is shown clearly by the liturgical composition quoted in Col 1:15-20" (p. 211).

Pokorny, Petr. *Colossians: A Commentary.* Peabody: Hendrickson, 1991. Pokorny notes the tension that exists between the hymn's view that the "superhuman powers" are good and the letter writer's view in Colossians 2 that they are defeated opponents and instruments of sin: "The theology of Colossians is not a systematic work" (p. 142).

Schweizer, Eduard. *The Letter to the Colossians: A Commentary.* Minneapolis: Augsburg, 1982. A superb, faith-filled commentary which explores Colossians 1:15-20 primarily from a philosophical perspective.

Schweizer, Eduard. *Jesus Christ: The Man from Nazareth and the Exalted Lord.* Macon: Mercer University Press, 1987. Schweizer's chapter, "The Hymns in the New Testament," has a particular emphasis on Colossians 1:15-20 (pp. 24–25).

Vawter, Bruce. "The Colossians Hymn and the Principle of Redaction." *Catholic Biblical Quarterly* 33 (1971) 62–81. Vawter makes the good point that the author of Colossians cited the hymn of Colossians 1:15-20 because he agreed with its theological content.

Wedderburn, A.J.M. "The Theology of Colossians." *The Theology of the Later Pauline Letters*. New Testament Theology Series. Cambridge: Cambridge University Press, 1993. (See pp. 1–71, esp. 64–71, on "The Continuing Influence of Colossians.")

Wilder, Amos N. *Early Christian Rhetoric: The Language of the Gospel*. Cambridge: Harvard University Press, 1971. A revolutionary book which highlights the wealth of insight to be gained from a literary rather than an historical approach to the New Testament.

Wink, Walter. *Naming the Powers: The Language of Power in the New Testament*. Philadelphia: Fortress, 1984. This is volume one in Wink's three-volume series on "The Powers" and contains excellent linguistic studies which lay the foundations for the interpretations he expounds in volume two, *Unmasking the Powers* (1986), and volume three, *Engaging the Powers* (1992), also published by Fortress. The first volume was largely written in reaction to the monograph of Wesley Carr, in which Carr argued that the author of Colossians views "the principalities and powers" in Colossians 2:10 and 2:15 as good. See Wesley Carr, *Angels and Principalities: The Background, Meaning and Development of the Pauline Phrase HAI ARCHAI KAI HAI EXOUSIAI*. Society of New Testament Studies Monograph Series 42. Cambridge, England: Cambridge University Press, 1981.

Wink, Walter. "The Hymn of the Cosmic Christ." *The Conversation Continues: Studies in Paul & John In Honor of J. Louis Martyn*. Eds. Robert T. Fortna and Beverly R. Gaventa, 235–45. Nashville: Abingdon, 1990. Explores the parallels between Colossians 1:15-20 and the *Tripartite Tractate* from Nag Hammadi. More importantly, Wink ends with some challenging contemporary reflections on Colossians 1:15-20.

Wright, N. T. "Poetry and Theology in Colossians 1.15-20." *New Testament Studies* 36 (1990) 444–68. I agree with Wright about the integral, nonredacted nature of Colossians 1:15-20 and have benefited from the richness of his Christological reflections.

Yates, Roy. *The Epistle to the Colossians*. Epworth Commentaries. London: Epworth, 1993. In this popular work, Yates often offers solid commentary, but agrees with the view of Wesley Carr that the author of Colossians views "the powers and principalities" of Colossians 2:10 and 2:15 as good. See above under Wink, *Naming the Powers*.

Universal Reconciliation in Christ Jesus

VI-1. Ephesians 2:14-16—
The Cross of Christ Reconciles All

A. TRANSLATION AND STRUCTURAL ANALYSIS

2:14 For he is our peace,
> *having united* **both into one,**
> and *having torn down* the dividing wall of hostility,
> in his flesh,

2:15 *having abolished* the law with its commandments and legal claims,
> so that he might create in himself **one** new humanity out of **the
> two,**
> thus *effecting* peace,

2:16 and might reconcile **both** with God, in **one** body, through his cross,
> *having slain* the hostility on it (NAB adapted).

Many commentators divide the Letter to the Ephesians, written by
a Jewish Christian disciple of Paul between 80-100 C.E., into two
parts. Chapters 1–3 mainly detail what God has done for the
Ephesians, former Gentile non-believers, and share many charac-
teristics of a letter of congratulations. Chapters 4–6 are exhortatory.
  Ephesians 2:14-16 occurs in the congratulatory section of
Ephesians and is unique to its context in a number of ways. First,
it celebrates what Jesus Christ has done and not what God has

done as is the case with the rest of Ephesians 1–3. Second, it breaks the train of thought in Ephesians 2:11-22. See, for example, how the contrast, introduced in 2:13 between those who are "far off" and those who are "near," is first resumed in 2:17. Third, there is a certain parallelism between the lines. I have indicated with bold print the contrast between both/two and one. As I will argue later on in this chapter, this contrast includes all reality: unity between heaven and earth; unity between Jews and Gentiles; unity between all people and God. Fourth, 2:14-16 is constructed out of eight verbs, five of which are participles and are italicized in the text I've presented. Fifth, there is the tension between violent and positive vocabulary. I would classify the following words as violent: tore down, dividing wall, hostility (twice), abolished, through his cross, having slain. Among positive words I would include: peace (twice), united, create, one new humanity (one body), effect peace, reconcile. Borrowing my classification of parallelism from number three, I would suggest that we have the following pattern: 2:14 has positive/negative; 2:15 has negative/positive/positive; 2:16 has positive/negative. And if we really wanted to be complete, the pattern has one additional refinement: 2:14 has "hostility" at its end and so does 2:16.

My purpose in the previous paragraph was not to overwhelm my readers with the intricate construction of Ephesians 2:14-16. Rather, I had a more simple aim: I wanted to illustrate in my own way what many scholars have been saying for the last thirty years or so, that Ephesians 2:14-16 is a hymn. One can consult Andrew Lincoln (1990, 127–28) and Markus Barth (1974, 6–8) for more scholarly detail on how one detects the presence of a hymn through the participles used in the passage, constructions such as parallelisms, and disruptions in the flow of thought. Incidentally, and for the same reasons given in great detail at the beginning of my chapter on Colossians 1:15-20, I treat the hymn of Ephesians 2:14-16 as integral. That is, I can make good sense out of it as it is and do not presuppose that the author of Ephesians redacted it by adding such phrases as "through the cross." For a different view see Lincoln (1990, 128).

Let me adapt an observation made by Romano Penna (1988, 139) to help my readers make greater sense out of what, at first, may be a bewildering array of terms in Ephesians 2:14-16. I suggest that we approach each of the three lines of the hymn with three questions. First, what was the previous nature of duality which these lines treat? Second, how has Christ rectified the previous condition? Finally, what is the result of Christ's salvific action? In the sections that follow I will have the opportunity to explore in greater depth the initial answers to these three important questions that might have come to mind.

I have looked high and low to find a hymn or poem that might help us visualize what the composer of Ephesians 2:14-16 had in mind in praising Christ our Peace. So many of the hymns about peace which I consulted were individualistic and of little, if any, benefit in helping us recapture the composer's vision of universal peace. Then one Sunday in Rome during morning prayer the following hymn was sung, which I have here freely translated into English:

> Oh, first and last day,
> day radiant and glorious
> of the triumph of Christ.
>
> The Risen Savior
> promulgates for all time
> the edict of peace.
>
> Peace between heaven and earth,
> peace between all peoples,
> peace in our hearts.
>
> The paschal alleluia
> resounds throughout the Church
> journeying through the world.
>
> Gathered for praise,
> harmonious and perennial,
> in the assembly of the saints.
>
> To you, O Christ, be glory,
> power and honor
> world without end. Amen (Fourth Sunday, Italian breviary).

This hymn is helpful, for it celebrates the multileveled peace which Christ our Savior has effected for us. If we would expand its third stanza and downplay its personalistic dimension, we would create what Ephesians 2:14-16 is proclaiming: Peace between heaven and earth; peace between Jew and Gentile; peace between all peoples. There is a further contrast between this hymn at morning prayer and the Ephesians hymn. The hymn on Sunday, the day of the Lord's resurrection, highlights the power of the Risen Christ. Ephesians 2:14-16, on the other hand, stresses Christ's violent death. See "in the flesh" (2:14) and "through the cross" (2:16). Note also that 2:13 has "through the blood of Christ."

Having come to appreciate somewhat the artistry and thought patterns of the composer of the hymn of 2:14-16, let's take a brief look at the contexts into which the author of Ephesians has set the hymn. Just as a glorious setting can enhance the brilliance of a diamond, so too can literary settings enhance the spectacular character of this early church hymn to Christ our Peace.

B. The Context

The *immediate context* of Ephesians 2:14-16 is 2:11-12 and 2:17-22, and clearly shows that at a very basic level the author of Ephesians wanted the hymn to refer to the unity which Christ, the bringer of peace and reconciliation, has brought to Jew and Gentile. What the Gentiles were "at one time" (2:12), they are "no longer" (2:19) because of Christ. Although "at one time" the Gentiles "were alienated from the community of Israel" (2:12), now they are "no longer strangers and sojourners, but are fellow citizens with the holy ones and members of the household of God" (2:19). Jews, who once regarded Gentiles as unclean and "without God" (2:12), now form one body with them. Gentiles, who once viewed Jews as so different as to be haters of humanity, are now part of the same temple with the Jews.

Besides stressing the new unity between Gentile Christians and Jewish Christians, the author of Ephesians 2:11-13, 17-22 also wants to show his readers, who are primarily Gentile Christians, that their salvation is part of a longer history, that of Israel. And behind this intention we can catch a glimpse of one of the major reasons why the author wrote Ephesians, namely, to show Gentile Christians that they had roots in God's prior salvation history.

Put another way, the author of Ephesians does not have the same problem which Paul had in writing Romans 9–11 wherein he had to deal with the arrogance of some Gentile Christians over against Israel (see especially Rom 11:12-20). Rather the author is addressing a situation wherein Gentile Christians are ignorant of their roots in Israel and need to be told whence they have come (Lincoln 1990, 133).

From the *broader context* I select two items. First is the theme of unity. If my readers have any doubt whatsoever that the author of Ephesians is concerned about unity, I refer them to 4:1-6, which is often used for liturgies during the Church Unity Octave from January 18–25. I quote the NAB: "I, then, a prisoner for the Lord, urge you to live in a manner worthy of the call you have received, with all humility and gentleness, with patience, bearing with one another through love, striving to preserve the unity of the spirit through the bond of peace: one body and one Spirit, as you were also called to the one hope of your call; one Lord, one faith, one baptism; one God and Father of all, who is over all and through all and in all." The unity between Jewish Christians and Gentile Christians is of a piece with the unity God has established in the Church.

The second point I draw from the total context of Ephesians has direct bearing on the meaning of 2:14, the hymn's first stanza, especially regarding the terms "both" and "tore down the dividing wall of hostility." My point is this: Christ has made peace between heaven and earth. ("Both" in Greek is the neuter *ta amphotera;* 2:15 has the masculine *tous dyo* and 2:16 has the masculine *tous amphoterous.*) And he has effected such peace by tearing down the wall of hostility between them. In "Key Concepts and Images" I will return to the various meanings proposed for "the wall." Here I concentrate on "hostility." It is my contention that "hostility" in 2:14 means not only the hostility occasioned between Jews and Gentiles because of the existence of the Law (see especially 2:15), but also the hostility which exists between humankind and the evil powers. Surely, God is not warring from heaven against humanity. As we will see from sample verses in Ephesians, it is the evil powers that are hostile to humans.

Like other New Testament documents, Ephesians has much to say about the evil powers. As a matter of fact, no New Testament hymnist or author, it seems, could make sense of our Savior Jesus Christ in an "age of anxiety" without relating Christ to the evil powers. Here are a few salient passages from Ephesians. Christ is seated at God's right hand in the heavens, "far above every principality, authority, power, and dominion, and every name that is named not only in this age but also in the one to come" (1:21). The author leaves no doubt as to who is Lord. Paul is a minister of God's mystery "hidden from ages past in God who created all things, so that the manifold wisdom of God might now be made known through the church to the principalities and authorities in the heavens" (3:9-10). We will return to this bold ecclesiological statement under "Reflection Starters" below. Finally, in 6:11-12 the author exhorts his readers to "put on the armor of God so that you may be able to stand firm against the tactics of the devil. For our struggle is not with flesh and blood but with the principalities, with the powers, with the world rulers of this present darkness, with the evil spirits in the heavens."

As a summary of the rich data in Ephesians about the evil powers, I make two brief observations, leaving certain details to our discussion of the image of "the wall" in the section on "Key Concepts and Images." First, there is no doubt that there is hostility between the evil powers and humans. Second, Christ has disarmed these evil powers through his death on the cross (see "in the flesh" of 2:14, which is parallel to "through his cross" in 2:16).

Now that we have reconnoitered the composer's universalist message of peace in 2:14-16, it is high time that we enter more fully into what it means to sing out with joy and confident conviction that Christ is our Peace. We will commence our section with the image of "the wall" and thus connect the discussion we have just concluded on the meaning of "hostility" in 2:14 with that powerful image.

C. KEY CONCEPTS AND IMAGES

I will consider two topics in this section: the wall and Christ our Peace. First, the wall. When the first line of the hymn of 2:14-16 mentions "the dividing *wall* of hostility," it is reveling in the fine art of ambiguity. That's right. I consider ambiguity to be praiseworthy

in a hymn. Put another way, the composer is not writing a set of
instructions on how to operate your new computer software program where ambiguity would be blameworthy—and maddening!
The composer is writing a hymn whose words can be ambiguous,
that is, they can admit of more than one meaning. Before I detail
three possible meanings for "the wall" of 2:14, let me say even
more about ambiguity. What I say at length here can also be ap-
plied to the other New Testament hymns treated in this book.

Perhaps one of the most famous examples in literature of ambiguity is found in Shakespeare's *Macbeth*. If you recall, the
witches predicted three things to Macbeth. First, he would be
king, but not a father of kings. Second, he would reign until
Birnam Wood marched to Dunsinane. Finally, no man born of
woman could vanquish him. As Macbeth finds out tragically, all
three predictions bear more than one meaning. That is, they are
ambiguous and fulfillable on at least two levels. As Macbeth
laments, "And be these juggling fiends no more believed, That
palter with us in a double sense" (V, 8, 19-20).

Recent studies on John's Gospel are familiarizing us with that
author's penchant for ambiguity. Of course, we may want to call
it "misunderstanding" or "irony," but the truth of the matter is
simple. Some Johannine statements are open to more than one
meaning. Consider, for example, John 3:3 where Jesus tells
Nicodemus: "No one can see the kingdom of God without being
born again (from above?)." See also John 4:32 and 19:30.

My final example is closer to home. I refer to Gerard Manley
Hopkins' poem, "Heaven Haven: A nun takes the veil." I will first
quote it and then give two interpretations which indicate its ambiguity.

> I have desired to go
> Where springs not fail,
> To fields where flies no sharp and sided hail
> And a few lilies blow.
>
> And I have asked to be
> Where no storms come,
> Where the green swell is in the havens dumb,
> And out of the swing of the sea.

The American composer Samuel Barber set this poem to music in his "Four Songs, Opus 13," having changed its title to "A Nun Takes the Veil: Heaven Haven." Barber's biographer, Barbara B. Heyman, maintains that Hopkins' poem "deals with the quest for solitude in nature, a subject close to Barber's heart and one that he would turn to many times in future works" (1993, 201–2). While Barber and Heyman's interpretations of Hopkins' poem may capture one of its dimensions, they fail to notice the irony which nuns, and indeed monks too, see in Hopkins' poem. If one is to be true to religious life, how does one avoid the spiritual storms which St. John of the Cross called "the dark night of the soul"? The nun, taking the veil, is seeking the impossible. Or expressed differently and in terms of my argument here, Hopkins' "Heaven Haven" is ambiguous, that is, open to more than one meaning.

Now that I have primed the pump for a consideration of the ambiguity of "the wall" in Ephesians 2:14, let's take a close look at the three interpretations which commentators usually present as possible meanings. As we begin, I remind my readers that "the wall" is modified by "hostility." That is, we will not be looking for a benign wall. As Markus Barth is keen to remind us, we are talking here about a wall comparable to the former Berlin Wall or Iron Curtain (1974, 263–64). In my own imagery, we are not talking about a friendly "dividing wall" like those around construction sites which are meant to protect us from harmful falling objects. Rather we are talking about walls which pen us in or keep us out and prevent us from going where we need to go or where God wants us to go.

The first example I give is of *a wall which separates heaven from earth*. This meaning of "the wall" corresponds well with what I said earlier about Christ and the evil powers. By his death "in the flesh" Christ has torn down the wall which separated heaven and earth (2:14). I quote from 1 Enoch, a document dated from between the second century B.C.E. to the first century C.E., which is attributed to the biblical figure Enoch who did not die but was taken up into heaven (see Gen 5:24): "And behold I (Enoch) saw the clouds: and they were calling me in a vision; and the fogs were calling me; and the course of the stars and the lightnings were rushing me and causing me to desire; and in the vision, the winds were causing me to fly and rushing me high up into heaven. And I kept coming (into heaven) until I approached a *wall* which was built of white marble and surrounded by tongues of fire; and it began to frighten me" (1 Enoch 14:8-9, emphasis mine).

The second example is of the *wall which separated the Court of the Gentiles from the Jerusalem Temple's inner courts and sanctuary.* Writing after the Jewish War when the Jerusalem Temple was destroyed, the Jewish historian Josephus twice mentions this wall (*Antiquities of the Jews* 15.11.5, and *Jewish War* 5.5.2). This was not an ordinary wall, but contained an inscription in various languages warning would-be Gentile trespassers that they would incur death if they violated the barrier. In 1871 "one of the pillars was found and on it was the warning inscription: 'No man of another race is to enter within the *fence and enclosure* around the Temple. Whoever is caught will have only himself to thank for the death which follows'" (Lincoln 1990, 141, emphasis mine). If Christ has united Jew and Gentile as seems clear in Ephesians 2:15, then the wall of this second example may help us interpret the meaning of "the wall" in 2:14.

The final example is drawn from the Jewish writing, *Letter of Aristeas,* which dates from the third century B.C.E. to the first century C.E. and describes *the Law as a fence.* Paragraph 139 reads: "In his wisdom the legislator, in a comprehensive survey of each particular part, and being endowed by God for the knowledge of universal truths, surrounded us with *unbreakable palisades and iron walls* to prevent our mixing with any of the other peoples in any matter, being thus kept pure in body and soul, preserved from false beliefs, and worshiping the only God omnipotent over all creation" (see also no. 142). This example shows clearly why the composer of the hymn of Ephesians 2:14-16 mentions "the law with its commandments and legal claims" (2:15) almost in the same breath as "the dividing wall of hostility" (2:14).

As I contemplate these three examples, I have the keen sensation in my scholarly being that I should argue vigorously for only one possible meaning of "the wall" in Ephesians 2:14. But that sensation needs to be ignored and overruled, for ambiguity and not univocity rules the day in poetry and hymns. So I instruct you, my readers, to frolic in faith in the rich and protean symbol of "the wall" in Ephesians 2:14. Indeed, it is true that Christ is our Peace because he has torn down the wall which the hostile evil powers had erected between heaven and earth. And indeed it is also true that Christ is our Peace because he has demolished the wall which separated Gentiles from worshiping the God of Abraham, Isaac, and Jacob. And indeed it is further the truth that Christ is our Peace because he has deconstructed the barrier of the Law which prevented Jews from freely sharing life with Gentiles. Let us rejoice and be glad because all this is what Christ's cross has accomplished!

These concluding remarks on the multilayered (ambiguous) meaning of "the wall" of Ephesians 2:14 have nudged us right up against our next topic—Christology. To it I now turn, and in doing so will provide answers to the three questions I raised earlier: (1) What was the previous condition of duality? (2) How did Christ rectify this condition? (3) What is the result of Christ's activity?

According to the hymn, *Christ has made peace on all levels,* whether between heaven and earth, Jews and Gentiles, humanity and God, or even humanity against itself. Christ has made them one. And Christ has made peace—has made them one—through some violent activities: he has torn down the dividing wall of hostility; he has abolished the law; he has slain hostility. Although commentators frequently ignore the hymn's references to Christ's violent actions or take them as parallels to his positive actions, they are so prominent as to call out for attention. I wonder whether these words of violence are meant to remind the readers/singers of this hymn that what Christ accomplished, whether by violent or pacific actions, he did through one of the most degrading and violent deaths known to antiquity—crucifixion. Notice how a reference to Christ's violent death on the cross opens and closes the hymn of 2:14-16: "in his flesh" (2:14) and "through his cross" (2:16).

Perhaps we can approach the centrality of the Cross in 2:14-16 from another angle. Is there a description of Christ's death in the Gospels or in Paul which approximates what 2:14-16 says about the universal peace effected by Christ's death? Maybe we can gain some insight by means of such a comparison. I offer the following examples and commence with Jesus' words in John's Gospel about the effects of his death: "And when I am lifted up from the earth, I will draw everyone to myself" (12:32). Surely, John teaches that there is a universal aspect to Jesus' death. Matthew 27:51, Mark 15:36, and Luke 23:45 narrate that the veil of the Temple sanctuary was torn into two from top to bottom at Jesus' death. So the Synoptics use powerful imagery to say that Gentiles now have access to God (without the Law?). And Matthew goes on to widen the effects of Jesus' death for those under the earth by writing: "The earth quaked, rocks were split, tombs were opened, and the bodies of many saints who had fallen asleep were raised" (27:52). Finally, Paul, in Romans 5:1, 10-11, has this to say about Christ's death on the cross: "Therefore, since we have been justified by faith, we have peace with God through our Lord Jesus Christ. . . . Indeed, if, while we were enemies, we were reconciled to God through the death of his Son, how much more, once reconciled, will we be saved by his life. Not only that, but we also boast of God through our Lord Jesus Christ, through whom we have now received reconciliation." Thus, Paul links together peace and reconciliation and comes very close to saying what one verse of our hymn, 2:16, says in hymnody.

From the passages I have quoted above, it seems clear that Paul and the evangelists capture some aspect of the meanings of 2:14-16, but all of them fall short of universalizing the effects of Christ's death on the cross the way the hymnist of 2:14-16 does. The results of Christ's ignominious death by crucifixion were the reconciliation of the cosmos, the reconciliation of Jews and Gentiles, the reconciliation between God and humanity, and the reconciliation of men and women. If I might state the obvious, what 2:14-16 trumpets regarding the universal effects of Christ's violent death on the cross is striking and somewhat unique.

If Christ's death on the cross has stamped out those things which stood in the way of reconciliation and peace, what have been its positive effects? Of these positive effects, I focus my attention on one: ". . . so that he might create in himself one new humanity out of the two" (2:15). Out of Jewish Christians and Gentile Christians Christ has created something new which is totally dependent on his graciousness. Let me skirt the edges of the meaning of this powerful image. Contrary to our North

American predispositions, the hymn does not celebrate individualism. Christ has created a community where people are one in their togetherness. In this the "one new humanity" of 2:15 is similar in meaning to what 2:16 means by "in one body"; that is, a worldwide Church has been created which lives from the life engendered by Christ's death on the cross.

Another approach to the meaning of 2:15 is to ascertain what Paul, the founder of the Pauline school in whose tradition Ephesians and the hymn of 2:14-16 stand, says about "new creation." There are two main passages in Paul, one of which also mentions "reconciliation." In Galatians 6:15 Paul concludes his argument with the feisty Galatians using this Christological aphorism: "For neither does circumcision mean anything, nor does uncircumcision, but only a new creation." In 2 Corinthians 5:17-19, a passage in which some commentators have detected the presence of a hymn, Paul writes: "So whoever is in Christ is a new creation: the old things have passed away; behold, new things have come. And all this is from God, who has reconciled us to himself through Christ and given us the ministry of reconciliation, namely, God was reconciling the world to himself in Christ, not counting their trespasses against them and entrusting to us the message of reconciliation."

To me these passages from Galatians and 2 Corinthians take on even greater significance when I realize that in a strand of Hellenistic Judaism, represented by the delightful religious romance *Joseph and Aseneth*, religious conversion was called "a new creation." Dated between the first century B.C.E. and the second century C.E., *Joseph and Aseneth* says this about the Egyptian Aseneth who had been idolatrous before her conversion and wanted to marry Joseph, a Jew and Pharaoh's right hand man: "Behold, from today, you will be renewed and formed anew and made alive again" (15:5). And in 8:11, Joseph's prayer for Aseneth's conversion contains these words: "Lord, bless this virgin, and renew her by your spirit, and form her anew by your hidden hand, and make her alive again by your life." If I view Ephesians 2:15 from the vantage points of Galatians 6:15, 2 Corinthians 5:17-19, and *Joseph and Aseneth* 8:11 and 15:5, then I realize that the hymnist is not saying that Christ has created something from what already is. Rather the community which Christ has fashioned by his costly Cross is so new that it is a *new* creation. In the words of Ralph P. Martin: ". . . a new entity is born that is not a revamped Judaism nor a patched-up paganism; it is the new creation that presages the 'reconciliation of all things' in God's kingly rule over all creation" (1981, 196).

Let me transpose the ancient symbol of conversion as new creation to our contemporary experience. Some of us have the new and powerful energy which surges through us when we undergo conversion. That experience is very much like being created anew, for we momentarily forget our physical and spiritual aches and pains and are ready to transform the entire universe with endless ebullience. And perhaps some of us, at one time or another, have also been present when an entire community has been swept up in the creative power of conversion. There is nothing else to do on those rapturous occasions than to break out in songs of praise to our Creator God and Redeemer, perhaps even to make merry to the strains of a hymn composed from the verses of Ephesians 2:14-16!

In conclusion to this discussion of the key image of "Christ our Peace," I return to the three questions which initiated this section. From a threefold duality Christ has saved us by breaking down the wall of hostility through his Cross and has created one new community out of Jew and Gentile. Another way of summarizing our discussion is to return to the parallelisms to which I directed your attention at the very beginning of this chapter. I borrow my image and some of my terminology from Markus Barth (1974, 291–92). In Ephesians 2:14-16, we are dealing with a braid made out of three strands. The beauty of the braid is that its strands form a harmonious whole. It is only by close inspection that one can detect the individual strands and the part each contributes to the beauty of the whole. The first strand highlights the peace which is only found in Christ: "Christ is our peace." The second strand accentuates how Christ achieved peace: "in his flesh," "in one body," and "through his cross." A third strand is formed by the verbs which describe Christ's actions. Although they are destructive to the obstacles of peace, Christ's actions are thoroughly constructive: he *unites* both into one; he *creates* one new humanity; he *effects* peace; he *reconciles* with God. And only for these constructive purposes does Christ tear down the wall, abolish the Law, and slay hostility.

D. REFLECTION STARTERS

The first of my four reflections harkens back to the festive ending of "Key Concepts and Images" in "Movement 2." When we experience the exhilaration of reconciliation in community, then we have glimpsed some of *the religious power* of the hymn of Ephesians 2:14-16. What 2:14-16 celebrates is almost too good to be true. As a matter of fact, daily existence seems to fly in the face of the event of universal reconciliation. But such reconciliation is true and often powerfully and experientially so in liturgy. Although he is describing the power of Ephesians' doxologies in general, what Andrew Lincoln writes has special bearing on 2:14-16: "As the writer encourages his readers to become caught up in doxology, he is reinforcing for them the Pauline gospel's alternative vision of existence in which Christ has triumphed over the powers and given all necessary resources to the Church" (1993, 144).

It would seem that Christian theology would welcome with open arms such New Testament hymns as Ephesians 2:14-16 which sing of Christ's universal reconciliation, especially in these days when there is such a great need for reconciliation among the Christian Churches, among warring nations, and between humankind and creation. Yet Ernst Käsemann has warned the Christian Churches to be very wary of the theology behind hymns like 2:14-16. In his own inimitable way he writes: "The message of reconciliation was taken up in primitive Christianity as one soteriological variant among others, and this occurred in that particular segment of the church which created hymns in praise of Christ as cosmic Victor. This involved, to be sure, utilizing a very dangerous theme. For one thing, the proclamation of an already accomplished reconciliation of the All rests on wildly enthusiastic presuppositions, just as it has repeatedly nourished such fanaticism right down to our own day" (1971, 60–61). As Käsemann makes clear in other sections of his provocative article, these hymns are dangerous, for they will lead Christians to believe that salvation is devoid of temptation and to "cease looking towards the future and giving (themselves) to the service of others" (pp. 55–56).

Since Käsemann is somewhat representative of a bevy of New Testament scholars who compare the Christology of Ephesians to that of the genuine Pauline letters and find it quite wanting, I cannot resist the temptation for one final quotation. The quotation has a significant bearing on the larger questions addressed by this book, namely, the existence, role, and control by contextualization of New Testament Christological hymns: "It is certainly striking that in the post-Pauline period the pre-Pauline tradition of the reconciliation of the All, uncontrolled by the doctrine of justification, can be taken up precisely by Paul's disciples" (1971, 63).

Am I saying more in this first reflection than that some people thrive on the doxological language of Ephesians, e.g., Ephesians 2:14-16, and some don't? I think I'm saying more. I am saying that hymns are not meant to prevent us from getting involved in the world. In Käsemann's terms, I would say that hymns, if taken seriously, should propel us back into the world for the service of our brothers and sisters. My reason for saying this is based on a profound principle of spirituality: you only sing truly that which you do. I will return to our need to be promoters of justice and peace in my second reflection.

I conclude my first reflection by asking how the Roman Catholic Church uses Ephesians at liturgy. According to my calculations of the lectionary and breviary, Ephesians 2:14-16 occurs twice. Its primary exposure is as part of the second reading (Eph 2:13-18) in the B cycle for Sunday of the Sixteenth Week. Its secondary exposure is as part of Ephesians 2:12-22 as the first reading in Year Two for Tuesday of the Twenty-ninth Week. For more frequently is Ephesians 1:3-10 (or parts thereof) used in liturgy. Although I do not consider Ephesians 1:3-10 a hymn, its doxological character and celebration of God's gracious will and purpose are fitting for Marian feasts like the Immaculate Conception and for the Evening Prayer of Saints, e.g., Evening Prayer I & II of the Common of Apostles. Frequently used, too, are Ephesians 2:19-22, e.g., Feasts of Apostles, and Ephesians 4:1-6, e.g., Votive Masses for the Unity of Christians. It seems to me that the liturgical use of Ephesians in the Roman Catholic Church highlights

God's utterly gratuitous love as in Mary's case, but also calls forth costly involvement in the world as witnessed, e.g., in the lives of the evangelizing apostles. Such liturgical usage challenges worshipers to imitate such evangelical stalwarts in the faith and also avoids Käsemann's biting critique because it encourages practice of what the Church sings.

My second reflection touches lightly on the area of *social justice,* for I have given extended consideration to such matters in the second and fourth reflections of my chapter on the hymn of Colossians 1:15-20, which also deals with the theme of reconciliation. I need but offer two observations here. From our earlier discussion of the wall of hostility, you may recall my insistence on the hostile intent of the "evil powers" or "principalities and powers." Andrew Lincoln succinctly summarizes for our contemporary concerns of justice and peace the arguments of Walter Wink about the "principalities and powers." He writes: Wink's arguments may enable "an analogy to be drawn between the cosmic principalities and powers and the systems, structures and institutions of our own day, which, within and beyond them, have a driving force for good or evil that is more than the sum of the effects of any individuals who may represent them or of any of their tangible manifestations" (1993, 158). If I might draw an example from my own backyard to explain what Lincoln and Wink mean, I would cite the way the O.F.M. branch of the Franciscan Order for a long time treated lay brothers as second-class citizens because they did not belong to the clergy. Surely our structure was good and was approved. But in fulfilling Vatican II's directive for religious to return to the charism of their founders, we Franciscans learned that we are all brothers first and that some of us brothers are priests. And of this writing I can state publicly that we are still trying to sort out all the justice and peace implications of our revised vision. Sometimes it takes decades and decades to make things right.

As long as I'm in a Franciscan modality, let me bring up my second observation which deals with "The Peace Prayer of St. Francis." When it seems almost impossible to achieve reconciliation on levels beyond our everyday personal relationships, this prayer offers considerable consolation and challenge without becoming individualistic or pietistic:

Lord, make me an instrument of your peace.
Where there is hatred, let me sow love;
where there is injury, pardon;
where there is doubt, faith;
where there is despair, hope;
where there is darkness, light;
and where there is sadness, joy.

O Divine Master, grant that I may not so much seek
to be consoled as to console,
to be understood as to understand,
to be loved as to love.
For it is giving that we receive,
it is pardoning that we are pardoned,
and it is in dying that we are born to eternal life.

While closely related to my second reflection, my third can
stand alone, for it more narrowly addresses the issue of *reconciliation between different groups.* One of the hallmarks of the theology
of reconciliation in Ephesians 2:14-16 is its teaching that Christ
has broken down one of the most violent discriminations known
to antiquity—that between Jew and Gentile. In Christ these two
enemies have become one. Should not what Christ has done for
Jew and Gentile be the model, verily the source, for the elimina-
tion of other divisions within humanity? In what follows I treat
two contemporary divisions.

In his excellent monograph on the history of the interpretation
of Ephesians 2:11-22, William Rader gives special attention to
the division between blacks and whites (his terminology). I sample one of his passages: "The peace made by Christ between Israel
and the Gentiles dare not be seen as only a parallel to peace between blacks and whites or other hostile groups, but as its source:
'only the peace between Jews and Gentiles, which makes both together have peace with God and free approach to God (2:16-18)
is the source from which peaceful coexistence at all levels of life is
to be drawn'" (1978, 245 quoting from Marcus Barth). Put another way, almost all blacks and whites are Gentiles, who were
once separated from the people of God. So whites are no different from blacks, for all need to be included through the costly
Cross of Christ into God's people (Rader 1978, 243).

It could be said that Paul exhausted himself and lost his life for the sake of the unity of Jew and Gentile under God's grace and not under the Law. The author of Ephesians has shown in his use of the hymn of 2:14-16 how he has carried on the theological torch of Paul in this matter. It has been rightfully observed that Paul spent so much of his thought, time, and energy on reconciling Jew and Gentile that he was not able to develop his vision and praxis in the area of the reconciliation of male and female. Thus, he was not able to develop in any systematic way the baptismal creed of Galatians 3:28: "There is neither Jew nor Greek, there is neither slave nor free person, there is not male and female, for you are all one in Christ Jesus."

In a feminist criticism of the author of Ephesians, who borrowed heavily from Colossians 3:18–4:1 in writing his own household code in Ephesians 5:22–6:9, E. Elizabeth Johnson observes: "Although the religious vision of equality between Jew and Gentile finds concrete expression in the Christian community with the author's blessing, any parallel equality between men and women remains a religious vision rather than a mark of everyday life in the home" (1992, 341). The interested reader will find more detail on a similar feminist critique of Colossians in my third reflection on the hymn of Colossians 1:15-20.

In summary, scholars like Rader and Johnson are calling upon today's Christian communities to find in the reconciliation effected by Christ our Peace the source of the reconciliation of other divisions, be these between Afro-Americans and whites or between men and women.

My fourth and final reflection ties together my previous three reflections and does so by reminding my readers of Ephesians 3:10 which I quoted earlier under the concept of "hostility." In that passage the unity of Jew and Gentile, achieved by Christ's death on the cross, is such "that the manifold wisdom of God might now be made known through the church to the principalities and authorities in the heavens." Such a role for the Church is awesome, for through its life of reconciliation it is to show to the powers that be that they have been defeated by Christ. To me no one has captured the meaning of Ephesians 3:10, within the total context of Ephesians, more clearly and powerfully than Andrew Lincoln, from whom I again, with deep gratitude, quote: "It is not by its preaching nor by its worship but by its very existence as the one new humanity out of Jews and Gentiles, overcoming the division within the old order, that the Church reveals to the hostile powers that their divisive regime is at an end. It serves as a reminder and pledge of the overcoming of all divisions when the cosmos is restored to harmony in Christ (cf. 1.10)" (1993, 94–95). What a provocative challenge for the Church! When disunity rather than unity parades down the Church's corridors, when self-aggrandizement and stodginess buttress up the old walls of hostility or erect new ones, and when we are paralyzed by the fear of the changes which unification might send rushing into our corporate lives, then we know that the "powers and principalities" are still in control. But when we take to heart in faith the vision of the hymn of Ephesians 2:14-16, when we cooperatively work to end racial, sexual, and ecclesiastical discrimination, and when we extend a caring hand to our environment, then we know that we have truly proclaimed and confessed that Christ is our Peace and has reconciled all to God. Amen. Alleluia!

Annotated Bibliography

Barth, Markus. *Ephesians: Introduction, Translation, and Commentary on Chapters 1–3.* Anchor Bible 34A. Garden City: Doubleday, 1974. This volume addresses all problems of interpretation. Barth is of the opinion that the hymn of Ephesians 2 runs from verse fourteen to verse eighteen.

Barth, Markus. "Traditions in Ephesians." *New Testament Studies* 30 (1984) 3–25. On pp. 9–12, Barth investigates the hymns of Ephesians and proposes criteria for discovering the presence of hymns. These criteria are similar to those he lists on pp. 6–8 of his aforementioned commentary. In this 1984 publication Barth remains of the opinion that Paul authored Ephesians.

Charlesworth, James H., ed. *The Old Testament Pseudepigrapha.* Vol. 2. Garden City: Doubleday, 1985. This volume contains fresh translations, introductions, and notes on the *Letter of Aristeas* and *Joseph and Aseneth* by R.J.H. Shutt and C. Burchard respectively.

Johnson, E. Elizabeth. "Ephesians." *The Women's Bible Commentary.* Eds. Carol A. Newsom and Sharon H. Ringe, 338–42. Louisville:

Westminster/John Knox Press, 1992. A brief, helpful commentary on a letter whose household code has been the object of much recent criticism.

Heyman, Barbara B. *Samuel Barber: The Composer and His Music.* New York: Oxford University Press, 1992. Detailed study of Barber's life as a composer.

Käsemann, Ernst. "Some Thoughts on the Theme 'The Doctrine of Reconciliation in the New Testament.'" *The Future of Our Religious Past: Essays in Honour of Rudolf Bultmann.* Ed. James M. Robinson, 49–64. New York: Harper & Row, 1971. A provocative article by a New Testament scholar who also maintained that Ephesians was representative of "Early Catholicism."

Lincoln, Andrew T. *Ephesians.* Word Biblical Commentary 42. Dallas: Word Books, 1990. I have learned much from this extensive commentary. Lincoln is of the opinion that Paul did not write Ephesians and that its author redacted the hymn of Ephesians 2:14-16.

Lincoln, Andrew T. "The Theology of Ephesians." *The Theology of the Later Pauline Letters.* New Testament Theology Series, 73–172. New York: Cambridge University Press, 1993. This clearly written volume has stimulated my thought and influenced me greatly, especially in its final chapter on "Critical Appropriation of the Theology of Ephesians" (pp. 142–66).

Martin, Ralph P. *Reconciliation: A Study of Paul's Theology.* New Foundations Theological Library, 157–98, 247–49. Atlanta: John Knox Press, 1981. An extensive treatment of Ephesians 2:12-19.

Penna, Romano. *La Lettera agli Efesini: Introduzione, versione, commento.* Scritti delle origini cristiane 10. Bologna: Dehoniane, 1988. Excellent commentary—Penna is of the opinion that Ephesians 2:14-16 is not a hymn.

Rader, William. *The Church and Racial Hostility: A History of Interpretation of Ephesians 2:11-22.* Beiträge zur Geschichte der biblischen Exegese 20. Tübingen: J.C.B. Mohr (Paul Siebeck), 1978. This monograph teaches much as it shows how Ephesians 2:11-22 has been interpreted over the centuries, e.g., in the twentieth century in Nazi Germany and apartheid South Africa.

VI-2. 1 Timothy 3:16—
The Universality of Salvation
in Christ Jesus

A. TRANSLATION AND STRUCTURAL ANALYSIS

Undeniably great is the mystery of *our Christian existence,*
  Who was manifestED *in* the flesh, (line 1)
  vindicatED *in* the spirit, (line 2)
  revealED to the angels, (line 3)
  proclaimED *in* Gentile groups, (line 4)
  believED *in* the world, (line 5)
  liftED up *in* glory (line 6) [NAB adapted].

I have adapted the NAB translation to bring out the eloquence of
the hymn's Greek formulation of praise to the exalted figure,
Jesus. Each past tense Greek verb in the six lines ends in -ed. I
have tried to express this bit of literary artistry, called *homoeoteleuton,* by capitalizing the endings of the English verbs. In
five of the six lines the author uses the same Greek preposition *en.*
In my translation I have tried to convey this phenomenon by
using "in" in each instance and italicizing each. While my translation of "in" captures one dimension of the composer's artistry, it
fails to do justice to the composer's ability in Greek to use one
preposition which has many meanings. Thus, line four is accurately translated as "preached *among* the Gentiles," and line five is
rendered correctly as "believed in *throughout* the world." The
English prepositions "among" and "throughout" derive from the
preposition *en,* which also occurs in lines one, two, and six, and is
translated "in" by most English versions. At this juncture I plant

a question in my readers' minds: Is it haphazard that the composer did not use the same Greek preposition *en* in line three: "revealed to the angels"? Perhaps, the composer could not find a Greek verb which could be fittingly used with the same preposition. Or perhaps the composer is calling the worshipers' attention to this singular line. I favor this last possibility and will exploit it later on in this chapter.

At the risk of overwhelming readers who may have little or no understanding of Greek, I mention another instance of the composer's cleverness with the Greek language. In creating the hymn of 1 Timothy 3:16, the composer has manifested considerable ingenuity in selecting six aorist verbs. This verb tense may be used in different ways to indicate that something is past. For example, the events in lines one through three are past and completed. In lines four and five, however, the composer has used the aorist to signal the first phase of a past action. Thus, one could justifiably translate line four as "has begun to be proclaimed to the Gentiles" and line five as "has begun to be believed in throughout the world." It seems to me that the composer took great delight in wordsmithing.

For those readers who think that I am being too clever in my treatment of the verbs in lines four and five, I refer them to a similar phenomenon in Luke 1:51-53 (Mary's *Magnificat*). The verbs "has shown might," "dispersed," thrown down from," "lifted up," "has filled," and "has sent away empty" are all inceptive past tense verbs. With the conception of Jesus, God has only begun to show might, disperse, etc. God has not accomplished all of these actions already. Let me reduce my grammar lesson to a lesson in spirituality. When Christians pray lines four and five, they are not praying about something that their ancestors did once and for all. Rather their praying implicates them in continuing and fulfilling what their ancestors began. Those who pray these lines knowingly commit themselves to proclaim the Gospel to all people throughout the world.

Scholars maintain that the composer of this hymn displayed great skill in arranging its lines. The first three lines may be arranged chronologically: the incarnation, then the resurrection, and finally the ascension. Others detect an arrangement by contrasts. Thus, flesh is contrasted with spirit; angels are contrasted with humans (Gentiles); the world is contrasted with heaven (glory). Some note a further, chiastic arrangement among the contrasts: flesh/Gentiles/world are linked together *(A)* and spirit/angels/glory are banded together *(B)*. Thus, line one is *A;* lines two and three are *B;* lines four and five are *A;* and line six is *B*. Two chiastic patterns would seem to emerge and overlap: *ABBA* (flesh-spirit-angels-Gentiles) and *BAAB* (angels-Gentiles-world-glory). I adopt Werner Stenger's way of displaying the chiastic *ABBA* and *BAAB* patterns:

What is one to make of all these possible arrangements? In my opinion it may be that *all* of the above arrangements, plus even some others, provide structures by which we can arrive at an acceptable interpretation of the hymn. The composer's clever way of giving the preposition *en* at least three different meanings in five lines, and the composer's use of the aorist tense in different ways suggest to me that the composer might also have exercised theological and artistic wit in setting multiple arrangements for the hymn. In my detailed comments later I will play out two of the multiple arrangements possible for this hymn. My readers may want to try their own hands at finding other possible arrangements of this keenly wrought hymn.

I conclude this intensive section on the artistry of the composer of the hymn of 1 Timothy 3:16 with two quotations from the "Easy Essays" of Peter Maurin. They show how witty, philosophical, and artistic we can be in our own idiom. Perhaps we might allow the composers of New Testament hymns their own brand of artistic and theological ingenuity.

> The world would become better off
> if people tried to become better.
> And people would become better
> if they stopped trying to become better off.

They say that I am crazy
because I refuse to be crazy
the way everyone else is crazy (Ellsberg 1992, xxv).

The attentive reader will note that Maurin used *homoeoteleuton* in composing these "Easy Essays." Thus, the lines of the first essay all end with "better," and the lines of the second essay with "crazy." Also I draw your attention to Maurin's use of contrast in his first essay. We can recognize with delight the ABBA pattern of this contrast. Finally, these essays may take on greater meaning for my readers when I share with you some of Peter Maurin's background (see my chapter on "Let's Do A Background Check" for the importance of ascertaining backgrounds). Along with Dorothy Day, Maurin founded the Catholic Worker Movement in the United States and battled incessantly against capitalism and its evil of nurturing greed among its proponents. The reader might profitably consult 1 Timothy 6:6-10 and 17-19 to espy what the author of the Pastoral Epistles teaches about wealth.

B. THE CONTEXT

The *immediate* context in which the hymn of 1 Timothy 3:16 occurs helps us interpret it. The author who writes the Pastoral Epistles in Paul's name is very much concerned with what Christians profess as their faith and how they practice that faith in their daily lives. Not only does the author of these epistles quote a hymnic profession of faith in 1 Timothy 3:16 for his readers, but also does so in other hymns and creeds, e.g., Titus 3:4-7, whose interpretation will occupy us in another chapter. These hymns and various exhortations about an honorable life show the readers what it means to live as members of "the household of God" (1 Tim 3:15).

Put another way, the author of the Pastorals uses the traditional hymn of 1 Timothy 3:16 to argue against the opponents of the faith and to show his readers how "undeniably great is the mystery of their Christian existence." And despite the stereotyped nature of the author's polemic, the author does provide us with the general contours of what the opponents taught. They were against

God's creation. Specifically, they banned material goods like food and physically affective enjoyments like sexual intercourse in marriage. 1 Timothy 4:1-5, which occurs right after the hymn of 3:16, describes the tenets of the opponents and thus spotlights a cardinal background for the interpretation of the hymn: "Now the Spirit explicitly says that in the last times some will turn away from the faith by paying attention to deceitful spirits and demonic instructions through the hypocrisy of liars with branded consciences. *They forbid marriage and require abstinence from foods that God created* to be received with thanksgiving by those who believe and know the truth. For everything created by God is good, and nothing is to be rejected when received with thanksgiving, for it is made holy by the invocation of God in prayer" (emphasis mine). Salient portions of the hymn in 3:16 are diametrically opposed to the anticreation tenets of the opponents. For Jesus came in the "flesh" or human condition, and the good news is preached and believed in the reality of this world among the Gentiles (lines one, four, and five).

In the context of the Pastoral Epistles I note that the author is keen to express the universality of salvation. For example, he writes in 1 Timothy 2:4: God "wills everyone to be saved and to come to knowledge of the truth." And in painting the picture of Paul which he wants future generations to remember, the author emphasizes that the Jew Paul was called by God to be the apostle to the Gentiles (see, e.g., 1 Tim 2:7). Thus, the author interprets by Paul's life and teaching lines four and five of the hymn of 1 Timothy 3:16: "proclaimed to the Gentiles; believed in throughout the world."

C. Key Concepts and Images

Before I play out two possible interpretations of the arrangement of the hymn, I want to caution my readers that this hymn says nothing about the salvific character of Jesus' death as an expiation or ransom for human sins. The composer of the hymn locates salvation elsewhere in the Christ event. Also I challenge my readers to discern from the contours of the hymn what its composer thought was wrong with the cosmos. That is, why was

Christ manifested in the flesh, vindicated in the spirit, and revealed to the angels? Why is Christ preached among the Gentiles and believed in throughout the world? One interpretation of the arrangement of the hymn maintains that what was wrong with the world was its disunity and alienation. Christ has united earth and heaven and made all women and men beneficiaries of this good news. The "household of God" must proclaim this good news to the world through their good deeds and through the witness of their faith. The second interpretation has much in common with the first but finds the ultimate cause of the world's woes in evil angels. That is, it finds the core of the hymn in line three, "revealed to the angels." I now turn to these two interpretations of our composer's masterpiece.

From authors as conservative as Robert H. Gundry to those as liberal as Martin Dibelius and Hans Conzelmann, one finds acceptance of the first interpretation, that the hymn deals with the universality of salvation. Gundry writes: ". . . the Saviour has reunited heaven and earth" (1970, 207). In the view of Martin Dibelius and Hans Conzelmann, the juxtapositions or contrasts of the hymn seem to emphasize the universality of the saving event throughout all cosmic regions. Proclamation and faith itself are included in the salvation event (1972, 61–63). In this interpretation prime consideration is given to the hymn's three contrasts which I illustrated in the first part of this chapter. The salvation in Jesus Christ has touched all realms, reuniting what was alienated. The first contrast in lines one and two is interpreted from the widely attested Old Testament background found, for example, in Isaiah 31:3: "The Egyptians are human, not God, their horses are flesh, not spirit." In the synonymous parallelism of this verse we can ascertain that the realm of God is "spirit" and that the realm of the human is "flesh." That is, flesh is humankind seen from its weak, transitory, fragile situation. Where God is, there is the breath of life and power and eternity.

I take the risk of shipping crude oil to Saudi Arabia when I remark again that while lines one and two may include the entire compass of Jesus' earthly life, they say nothing explicitly about Jesus' salvific death. A key to the soteriological significance of these lines is the verb "vindicated" in line two. Philip H. Towner

presents a helpful interpretation of the meaning of "vindicated."
He observes: ". . . the occasion of Christ's vindication was his
resurrection/exaltation, at which point he was 'vindicated' before
hostile powers, whether human or angelic. . . . Thus line 2 affirms that upon entering the supernatural sphere through resurrection, Christ received vindication" (1989, 91). Towner's view
prepares us for examining the next contrast, "angels/Gentiles,"
found in lines three and four.

Lines three and four further the hymn's message that salvation
in Jesus Christ has significantly touched all realms. Not only has
the event of Christ Jesus involved the human realm (see "flesh" in
line one), but it has also had ramifications for the angelic realm.
Again Philip Towner's observations are on target: ". . . the NT
knows of and expresses in several ways the event of Christ's triumphant 'appearance' before angelic powers, though it is not always clear whether the powers envisioned are hostile or not (cf.
Phil 2:9-11; Col 2:15; Eph 1:21; Heb 1:3-4; 1 Pet 3:22; Rev 5:8-
14). And almost certainly it is to this tradition . . . that line 3 belongs" (1989, 92). Put another way, Towner sees line three as a
continuation of the meaning of line two which championed
Christ's "vindication" over hostile powers. In my second interpretation of the hymn I will return to Towner's insightful remarks.

In contrasting "angels" (line three) with "Gentiles" (line four),
the composer alludes to another dimension of the universality of
Jesus' salvation. For Jesus was "manifested in the flesh" not only
for the chosen people, the Jews, but also for the Gentiles. Put another way, the world is no longer separated along the lines of
those who are chosen and those who are not. Salvation is universal. Such an understanding is deeply Pauline, for his Law-free
gospel was for all Gentiles (see Rom 1:5). And as we saw in considering the larger context of this passage in the Pastoral Epistles,
this understanding is also that of the author of the Pastoral
Epistles (see, e.g., 1 Tim 2:7).

The final contrast is that of "world/glory" found in lines five
and six. Believers are not only to be found in some small territory
in the Middle East, but can be located throughout the world (*kos-
mos* in Greek). And Jesus is now in God's realm, the realm of
glory where there is endless power for good.

In summary, this first interpretation of the hymn accentuates the universality of the Christ event. This saving event has touched earth and heaven. Its message is for both Jew and Gentile. It has not been confined to some small spot of the world, but has been carried forth to the entire world. Where once disunity and huge barriers existed, now there exist unity and free access. But who or what has created the disunity or erected such huge barriers? In the second interpretation I will suggest an answer to this important soteriological question as I try to probe more closely into what has set up the hymn's three contrasts in the first place.

My second interpretation of the hymn's arrangement maintains that there is unity between earth and heaven because Christ has conquered the evil angelic powers. I begin by offering a different analysis of the hymn's structure, dividing it into two three-line "stanzas":

> Who was manifested in the flesh
> vindicated in the spirit
> revealed to the angels
>
> proclaimed in Gentile groups
> believed in the world
> lifted up in glory.

What are my reasons for such an analysis? I offer two which are based on the fundamental observation that each stanza stems from a different pattern of explaining what salvation involves. First, and relative to the second stanza, I find it parallel to the longer ending of Mark's Gospel. Mark 16:15, 16, 19 present the only place in the New Testament where such ideas are concentrated as proclamation of the good news, world-wide belief, and Jesus' ascension into heaven: "Jesus said to them [the Eleven], 'Go into the whole world and proclaim the gospel to every creature. Whoever believes and is baptized will be saved. . . . ' So then the Lord Jesus, after he spoke to them, was taken up into heaven." It seems to me that the same threefold concentration lies behind lines four through six of 1 Timothy 3:16. Expressed differently, my view is able to explain "lifted up in glory," which always seems redundant and out of chronological sequence after line two's "vindicated in the spirit" and line three's "revealed to the angels."

"Lifted up in glory" has its origins in a different way of patterning the salvation event. In this pattern Jesus, lifted up in glory, displays his salvific power through those who preach his good news to others and through those who believe in him and are thereby saved. I conclude my first point by suggesting that the content of the first stanza may well be that which is "proclaimed among the Gentiles and believed in throughout the world."

What possible reasons can I give for aggregating lines one through three into one stanza? First, as I stressed earlier in this chapter, line three is the only line of this artistically wrought hymn which lacks the Greek preposition *en*. It is surely possible that the composer is drawing our attention to that line by means of this exception. Second, as I've accentuated in my chapter on backgrounds, people of the first centuries lived in "an age of anxiety." Saviors, be she Isis or be he Christ, were only saviors insofar as they had conquered the evil angelic forces or were being worshipped by angelic forces. Let me expatiate on this second reason.

In dealing earlier with the universalist interpretation of this hymn, I noted Philip Towner's opinion that line two means Jesus was vindicated before hostile powers, whether human or angelic (1989, 91); and that line three "almost certainly" belongs to the tradition of "Christ's triumphant 'appearance' before angelic powers" as found in New Testament passages like Philippians 2:9-11 and 1 Peter 3:22 (1989, 92). Here is how the final lines of the hymn in Philippians express salvation in Christ Jesus: "Because of this, God greatly exalted him (Christ Jesus) and bestowed on him the name that is above every name, that at the name of Jesus, *every knee should bend of those in heaven and on earth and under the earth* and every tongue confess that Jesus Christ is Lord, to the glory of God the Father" (emphasis mine). And the final line of the hymn in 1 Peter 3:22 gives voice to salvation in Jesus Christ "who has gone into heaven and is at the right hand of God, *with angels, authorities, and powers subject to him*" (emphasis mine). To Jesus Christ as Savior, both good and malevolent angelic powers are subject.

In my chapter on the hymn of 1 Peter 3:18-22 I will call upon the writings of First and Second Enoch for interpretive background material on how Jesus the Savior is exalted above the angels. Here I allude to a different background to illustrate the so-teriological significance of line three of 1 Timothy 3:16. In the *Apocryphon of John*, which pertains to the Nag Hammadi materials, a female salvation figure, Pronoia, descends thrice to rescue her offspring. On her final trip she says: "Arise and remember that it is you who hearkened, and follow your root, which is I, the merciful one, and guard yourself against the *angels of poverty and the demons of chaos* and all those who ensnare you, and beware of the deep sleep and the enclosure of the inside of Hades" (Robinson 1990, 122, emphasis mine). The only point I garner from this parallel is the common element between line three of 1 Timothy 3:16, Philippians 2:9-11, 1 Peter 3:22, and the *Apocryphon of John:* the savior is more powerful than angelic forces. In his exaltation to the realm of the Spirit, Jesus Christ has revealed himself to the angelic forces as their ruler; and as their ruler, Jesus Christ is our Savior. In the logic of the soteriology our composer uses to speak to people who live in "an age of anxiety," lines one and two lead to and find their completion in line three. To be Savior, Jesus Christ must not only have been vindicated in the Spirit, he must have vindicated the spirits.

I now summarize my position. Lines one through three form a pattern of salvation quite different from lines four through six. In lines one through three we catch a glimpse of an answer to the question I posed earlier, that is, who or what has created the disunity or division we experience? The answer, we have concluded, is the evil angelic powers. In my treatment of 1 Peter 3:18-22 we will read how the composer of another New Testament hymn gives far greater specificity to this answer.

Am I reading too much into lines one through three? I readily concede that I am making theological points which are not immediately evident to the reader. What I am engaged in is called the art of interpretation. While it is an art, it is not totally creative. For I am bound by the science of setting the hymn against a certain set of historical and intellectual backgrounds. Besides the background of the letter in which the hymn is utilized, there are the backgrounds of the other New Testament hymns and the thought worlds of the composer's time. Given all that, I remark that my major reason for interpreting lines one through six of

1 Timothy 3:16 the way I have is to determine why and how Jesus is Savior.

D. REFLECTION STARTERS

My first reflection concerns the stress which line one places upon *the goodness of God's material creation*. The Savior "was manifested in the flesh," and all creation, including marriage and food, are good (1 Tim 4:1-5). Throughout the centuries, Christians have had to struggle to keep faith with this cardinal truth. Yes, our body is good and beautiful. Marriage and children are marvelous. Human culture and the city here below are things of wonder.

A second reflection picks up the dimension of *universality* which cascades and crisscrosses through the chiasmic contrasts of the hymn. Salvation in Jesus affects the entire universe and each and every individual in it. Again this is a truth with which the Church has wrestled for ages as it has combated prejudices of various sorts within and outside its ranks. The reader can surely add to the three prejudices I mention here: Gentiles against Jews, Catholics against Protestants, rich people against poor people.

A third thought deals with *evangelization* and takes its origin from lines four and five of the hymn and from the way these lines are used to interpret the entire hymn at Evening Prayer I on the Feast of the Epiphany and at Evening Prayer II on the Feast of the Transfiguration of Jesus, in the Roman Catholic Liturgy of the Hours. For both evening prayers, the entire hymn is set off in three stanzas of two lines each with the interpretive refrain: "Praise the Lord, all you nations." Thus, those who pray are invited to praise the Lord for the salvation proclaimed in the hymn and to become participants in proclaiming that salvation to all nations. For as we saw earlier in this chapter, the events of being "proclaimed" and "believed in" are not fully accomplished. They are continual and are to be continued by today's communities of believers.

Almost as an aside and in my quest to teach methodology to my readers, I call their attention to the phenomenon that the refrain at evening prayer is another example of how context aids interpretation of New Testament hymns. In this instance, by being encapsulated in the refrain, lines four and five of the hymn inter-

pret the entire hymn. And in its turn, the refrain itself is interpreted by the feasts themselves, for Epiphany celebrates Jesus'
manifestation to the nations (the magi) and the transfigured Jesus
has meaning not just for his Jewish disciples, but transcends that
earthly and ethnic context and is for all peoples. Such contextualization of the hymn of 1 Timothy 3:16 focuses on one aspect of
the universality of Jesus Christ. Perhaps, in a different liturgical
context, the spotlight might illumine line three: the power of
Jesus Christ over angelic powers, be they benign or hostile.

A final consideration has to do with *how Jesus Christ is Savior
for us*. Some fifty-five years ago Rudolf Bultmann, one of the
most influential New Testament scholars of the twentieth century, did New Testament interpreters a great service and a greater
disservice when he called for the de-mythologizing of the New
Testament. He benefited New Testament research by calling attention to the need to re-interpret for modern men and women
New Testament views on heaven and hell, demons and angels.
Bultmann's disservice stemmed from his inadequate views on the
nature and function of myth and consisted in leaving in his readers' minds the distinct impression that myth meant falsehood.

In two publications John L. McKenzie (1985; 1990) has made
available to a general audience much of recent research on the nature and function of myth. Mythmaking is a narrative way of
thinking which attempts to "explain" the ultimate realities of existence: What is the origin of evil? Does God exist? Is there an after-
life? Why do human beings exist? Myth "seeks to impose
intelligible form upon the realities that transcend experience. . . .
Myth presents in a story the constant reality of the universe. It
does not pretend that the symbol is the reality, but it proposes the
symbol as that which affords an insight into a reality beyond
understanding. The goal of mythopoeic thinking is truth, not
falsehood . . ." (McKenzie 1990, 77:24). Interested readers might
refer to the detailed articles by Robert A. Oden, Jr., and Fritz Graf
on "Myth and Mythology" (1992) which demonstrate how the
understanding of myth found in McKenzie's writings is generally
accepted in biblical studies today. For our purposes it is vitally important for readers to try to remember that myth, when used in
biblical studies, is a technical term and to try to neutralize the

common American view that "myth means falsehood." Also to be remembered is that Christian mythopoeic thinking deals with Jesus Christ, who was born of a woman and born under the Law (Gal 4:4). See also how the first line of 1 Timothy 3:16 gives witness to this fact that our Savior Jesus Christ was rooted in history.

When the composer of 1 Timothy 3:16 wanted to give expression to the faith of the Christian community that their Lord Jesus Christ was their savior because he had conquered the forces of evil, he used the means he had at hand—a truth-filled narrative which told of Jesus' revelation to the evil powers that he is their Lord: "he was revealed to the angels." I refer interested readers to the last two sections of my chapter on Colossians 1:15-20 and to my Conclusion for further reflections about the process of myth-making and how we moderns might get in contact with the Truth being expressed through such hymns as 1 Timothy 3:16.

As I look at the truth-filled narrative of lines one through three of 1 Timothy 3:16, I articulate some of its profound soteriology in this way. Today it seems to me that we are frequently caught up with questions about whether we are ultimately in control of our lives or whether forces greater than we have us by the scruff of our necks and are directing us hither and yon. In other words, we are being forced to ask the question: Is the universe ultimately benign to us? Are we finally to conquer sickness, crime, and ignorance or are we to be overwhelmed by these malevolent powers? Is there some sort of security in our lives as we fear losing our jobs, having inadequate or no health care, and living longer and longer without a penny to our names? Some of us seek answers from the stars or the lottery. Some seek a safety/salvation net elsewhere as they opt out of life through drugs of one sort or another. Others of us seek an answer—and do so in sheer faith—in Jesus Christ, who has vanquished the malevolent forces which seek to destroy any meaning we might find and enjoy in our material creation and our fleshly participation in it.

Praise be to Jesus Christ, Savior of us all and Conqueror of the evil powers who would alienate us from you and our enjoyment of the goods of creation, in which you so delighted during your days "in the flesh."

ANNOTATED BIBLIOGRAPHY

Dibelius, Martin, and Hans Conzelmann. *The Pastoral Epistles: A Commentary on the Pastoral Epistles.* Hermeneia Commentary Series. Philadelphia: Fortress, 1972. A learned, concise commentary with plentiful and helpful references to non-biblical backgrounds.

Ellsberg, Robert, ed. *Dorothy Day: Selected Writings.* Maryknoll: Orbis, 1992. Ellsberg has a superb introduction (xv–xli) to the life and times of this modern day saint, who lived from 1897–1980.

Fowl, Stephen E. *The Story of Christ in the Ethics of Paul: An Analysis of the Function of the Hymnic Material in the Pauline Corpus.* Journal for the Study of the New Testament Supplement Series 36, 155–94. Sheffield: JSOT Press, 1990. A serious attempt to interpret Philippians 2:6-11, Colossians 1:15-20, and 1 Timothy 3:16 by means of their function in their larger contexts. Accordingly, the emphasis in 1 Timothy 3:16 on Jesus' manifestation "in the flesh" helps the author to counter the opponents' denial of the goodness of creation.

Gundry, Robert H. "The Form, Meaning and Background of the Hymn Quoted in 1 Timothy 3:16." *Apostolic History and the Gospel: Biblical and Historical Essays presented to F. F. Bruce on his 60th Birthday.* Eds. W. Ward Gasque and Ralph P. Martin, 203–22. Grand Rapids: Eerdmans, 1970. This is a foundational article on 1 Timothy 3:16, from which I have profited much, even and especially when I have disagreed with the author's positions.

Karris, Robert J. *The Pastoral Epistles.* New Testament Message. Wilmington: Michael Glazier, 1979. I am told by those knowledgeable in the field that this is a lively and excellent treatment for the general reader. And who am I to dispute the experts!?

McKenzie, John L. "Myth." *Dictionary of the Bible,* 598–600. Milwaukee: Bruce, 1965.

McKenzie, John L. "Aspects of Old Testament Thought." *New Jerome Biblical Commentary.* Eds. Raymond E. Brown, Joseph A. Fitzmyer, and Roland E. Murphy, 77:23–24. Englewood Cliffs: Prentice-Hall, 1990.

Oden, Robert A., Jr., and Fritz Graf. "Myth and Mythology." *The Anchor Bible Dictionary.* Vol. 4. New York: Doubleday, 1992. This entry is divided into three topics. Oden has authored materials on the first two, "Mythology" (pp. 946–56) and "Myth in the OT" (pp. 956–60). Graf has written materials on the third topic, "Myth in the Greco-Roman World" (pp. 961–65).

Robinson, James M., ed. *The Nag Hammadi Library in English.* 3rd. rev. ed. San Francisco: HarperSanFrancisco, 1990. Brief introductions and translations of the papyrus manuscripts found in Nag Hammadi, Egypt, in 1945. There are forty-five separate titles. The book has 549 pages.

Stenger, Werner. *Introduction to New Testament Exegesis,* 18–21, 123–32. Grand Rapids: Eerdmans, 1993. On these pages Stenger summarizes some of the findings from his German monograph on 1 Timothy 3:16: *Der Christushymnus in 1 Timothy 3,16. Ein Struckturanalytische Untersuchung.* Regensburger Studien zur Theologie 6; Frankfurt am Main/Bern: Peter Lang/Herbert Lang, 1977.

Towner, Philip H. *The Goal of Our Instruction: The Structure of Theology and Ethics in the Pastoral Epistles.* Journal for the Study of the New Testament Supplement Series 34, 75–119, especially 87–93. Sheffield: JSOT Press, 1989. Excellent materials on the contemporary discussion about the theology and meaning of the Pastoral Epistles.

Young, Frances. *The Theology of the Pastoral Letters,* 50–68, 95–96. New York: Cambridge University Press, 1994. A treasure trove of insights, one of which occurs on p. 96: these epistles "will ram home the well-known slogans and doxologies and confessions of faith which carry the proper understanding of the tradition received in scripture and from Paul."

VII. Movement 4

Christ Jesus, the Saving Bath, and the Fallen Angels

VII-1. Titus 3:4-7— The Saving Communal Bath

A. Translation and Structural Analysis

3:4 But when the kindness and generous love of *God our Savior* appeared,
3:5 not because of any **righteous deeds which we had done**
    but because of his mercy,
    he saved us through the bath of rebirth
    and renewal effected by the *Holy Spirit,*
3:6 whom he richly poured out on us through
    Jesus Christ our savior,
3:7 so that we, **having been made righteous by his grace,**
    might become heirs in hope of eternal life (NAB adapted).

The commentators are generally divided over the question of whether Titus 3:4-7 is a hymn. Let me marshal the observations which have led me to the conclusion that it is indeed a hymn. This little exercise will give interested readers an opportunity to review what I said in Chapter II about the criteria used by scholars to ascertain the presence of a hymn in the New Testament.

My first set of arguments is from authority. The editors of the New American Bible have indented Titus 3:4-7, thereby showing that in their judgment this passage is poetic/hymnic. Likewise, the editors of the twenty-seventh edition of the Greek New Testament *(Novum Testamentum Graece)* also indent Titus 3:4-7. The master scholar of hymns, Ralph Martin, includes Titus 3:4-7 among the "sacramental" hymns (1983, 19).

My second set of arguments deals with the text itself, which I will analyze according to the eleven criteria proposed by Markus Barth for detecting the existence of hymns in the New Testament (1974, 6–8). Although we may quibble over whether or not one or the other criterion applies to Titus 3:4-7, it is remarkable that this passage meets at least six of the eleven criteria. I will work through the six criteria I believe that Titus 3:4-7 meets. Under Barth's name in the Annotated Bibliography of this chapter I will list the remaining five criteria. Perhaps the interested reader might want to see to what extent Titus 3:4-7 fails to match those criteria.

The primary focus of Barth's third criterion is on the passage's use of verbs as aorist participles in relative clauses and in consecutive clauses. Titus 3:4-7 meets this criterion in the following ways. In 3:7 we find an aorist passive participle which I have translated "having been made righteous." Grammarians usually call this use of the passive voice "the theological passive," for it is a circumlocution for God's activity. In 3:5 and 3:6 we have relative clauses. Titus 3:7 is a consecutive clause. Thus, the majority of the verbs in Titus 3:4-7 emphasize what God has done for us—the bedrock of hymns.

Barth's fourth criterion is simply stated: "Those who benefit from God's mighty acts speak in the first person plural" (1974, 7). In our English translation the first person plural occurs in every verse of Titus 3:4-7 and does so a total of seven times.

Barth's sixth criterion has as its concern the presence of "unique words," e.g., the Greek *hapax legomena: "Hapax legomena* reveal that the author quotes from a tradition that makes use of other vocabulary than he is wont to employ when he formulates his own thoughts . . ." (1974, 7). The phrase "the kindness and generous love" occurs only here in the New Testament. Also, the word "rebirth" (Greek: *palingenesia*) occurs only here in Paul's letters. Matthew 19:28 contains the only other occurrence in the New Testament of this rare word, which is often rendered in

English by "in the new age" or something similar. Moreover, in the other Pauline letters there is no clear reference to the Trinity as one finds in Titus 3:4-7: God our Savior, Holy Spirit, Jesus Christ our Savior.

Simply stated, Barth's eighth criterion is that of artistic structure: "Elements of careful structure distinguish the piece in question . . . parallelism of members is discernible . . ." (1974, 8). At first blush it does not seem that there is any artistic structure to Titus 3:4-7. Surely, Titus 3:4-7 is not like 1 Timothy 3:16 or 2 Timothy 2:11-13, or other hymns in the Pastoral Epistles. But I would suggest to my readers that there is considerable "parallelism of members" in Titus 3:4-7.

I have tried to accentuate one level of such parallelism by means of italics and boldfaced print in my translation. The italics point out the Trinitarian nature of our hymn, which sings of what God our Savior, the Holy Spirit, and Jesus Christ our Savior have done for believers. A very informative parallel to this Trinitarian emphasis is found in a writing contemporary to the Pastoral Epistles, *1 Clement* 46:6: "Do we not have one God, and one Christ, and one Spirit of grace *poured out* upon us?" I have italicized the verb "poured out," which modifies "Spirit," because it is the same verb used in Titus 3:6 of the Holy Spirit. Thus, the first level of parallelism, which highlights the role of the Trinity in our salvation, comes from a tradition also evidenced in *1 Clement*. A second level of parallelism interprets the Trinitarian formula by means of a key Pauline teaching: our righteousness stems from God's mercy and not from our works. I have spotlighted this parallelism by means of boldfaced print. So, if we label the hymn's Trinitarian emphasis *A* and its Pauline emphasis *B*, we have the pattern *ABAB*. Further, if we label "bath of rebirth and renewal" *C* and consider it to be the center of the *ABAB* pattern, then we might see that Titus 3:4-7 has a somewhat chiastic structure which accentuates the "salvific bath." This structure might be expressed *ABCAB*.

It seems to me that there is a more subtle, but effective parallelism running through our hymn. Titus 3:4-6 sings mightily of God's salvation, almost setting up the realization in the hymn's singers that this salvation is an accomplished fact. But then Titus 3:7 crashes the hymn singers back to reality, for this salvation is only "in hope." If I might put this phase of the hymn's artistic structure into my own hymnic structure, I would select the call-response modality used in some spirituals. First, there is a series of questions, then a series of answers.

> Are we saved? Yes, God our Savior did it.
> Do we save ourselves? No, God does it freely.
> Are we saved? Yes, the Holy Spirit did it through Jesus Christ.
> Are we saved? Yes, Jesus Christ our Savior did it.
> Are we saved? Yes, we've been justified.
> Are we saved? Not yet, for through all this saving we have become heirs in hope of eternal life.

Could Paul have said it any better?! See, e.g., Romans 8:24: "For in hope we were saved" (see also Rom 5:9). The hymnist's artistic use of paradox in the hymn of Titus 3:4-7 might be favorably compared to the use of paradox in 2 Timothy 2:11-13. Perhaps it was characteristic of some hymns in the Pauline school to be fashioned by means of paradox, which can be defined as a person, thing, or situation exhibiting an apparently contradictory nature.

From my perspective and in conclusion to this point, Titus 3:4-7 does exhibit the artistic structure of a certain parallelism of members. Barth's ninth criterion seems to be met in Titus 3:4-7: "The text offers a summary of the message of Christ, the so-called kerygma, but shows no concern for historical accuracy" (1974, 8). Surely, the Pauline kerygma of salvation by God's free gift permeates Titus 3:4-7. Further, Titus 3:4-7 seems to be little concerned about historical accuracy. Since Titus 3:4-7 is used each year as the second reading for the Christmas Mass at Dawn, many of my readers may have been predisposed to see Titus 3:4 as a reference to the Incarnation and thus the beginning of an historical sequence culminating in what Jesus Christ did for us in his death and resurrection (Titus 3:6). But a reference to the Incarnation in Titus 3:4 does not seem likely, for Titus 3:5, which contains the finite verb that governs the "when" clause of Titus 3:4, speaks of salvation "through the bath of rebirth" and not through the Incarnation. Further, Titus 3:6 does not specify how Jesus Christ is our Savior.

Barth's eleventh criterion is this: "The content of a given passage interrupts the context" (1974, 8). In one sense, Titus 3:4-7 fits its context, for it provides the basis for the author's exhortations. That is, because God has been gracious to them (see Titus 3:4), Christians should be gracious and generous to others (see Titus 3:8). But in another sense, Titus 3:4-7 does not fit its context, for its understanding of "deeds" (Greek: *erga*) stems from the Pauline contrast between "righteousness by grace" and "righteousness by deeds" and is quite different from that of Titus 3:1 and 3:8 where "deeds" are the good deeds which benefit society.

In conclusion, it is my judgment that Titus 3:4-7 is a hymn because of reasons external to the text, but especially because of internal reasons. That is, Titus 3:4-7 meets six of the eleven "objective" criteria of Markus Barth, the most important of which are artistic (criteria nos. 7 and 8) and linguistic (criteria nos. 3, 4, 6). Recall that in chapter one I espoused Peter O'Brien's view that the criteria were primarily stylistic and linguistic.

Perhaps what I have just said about the hymnic nature of Titus 3:4-7 is well and good, but needs to be illustrated some more. I use for my illustration a comparison between Titus 3:4-7 and "A Litany," a text by Phineas Fletcher (1582–1650) which was set to music as a hymn by Sir William Walton:

> Drop, drop, drop, slow tears,
> And bathe those beauteous feet,
> Which brought from heaven
> The news and Prince of peace.
>
> Cease not, cease not, wet eyes,
> His mercy to entreat
> To cry for vengeance
> Sin doth never cease.
>
> Drop, drop, drop, slow tears,
> In your deep flood
> Drown all my faults and fears;
> Nor let his eyes see sin,
> But through my tears.

Allow me to give a brief analysis of this English hymn. In its first stanza it uses the image "Prince of peace" to refer to Jesus' coming to take away sin and establish peace. We may have to read the second stanza a couple of times to realize what it is saying, for it is complex. Perhaps it would have been easier for us if the author had straightforwardly said: "Sin never ceases to cry out for vengeance from God." The final stanza, composed not in four lines like the previous two stanzas, but in five lines, strongly gives voice to the hymn's dominant imagery: the shedding of tears.

Does this hymn express the totality of the mystery of God's gift of forgiveness and the human response of sorrow and penance? In no way. But it does a superlative job in making its point, that is, the need of human remorse for sin.

When we turn from Fletcher's "A Litany" to the hymn of Titus 3:4-7, we note that our New Testament hymn does not have three stanzas, but is one long sentence in Greek, a phenomenon reflected in our English translation. The main clause is found in the middle of verse five: "he saved us through the bath of rebirth and renewal by the Holy Spirit." That is, all of the weighty theological content of the other verses is dependent on this main clause. In "A Litany" we look, almost in vain, for a subject, for this hymn has personified something material—tears. Of course, these tears are human tears as the last two words of the entire hymn state: "*my* tears." Yet my point stands that "A Litany" achieves its effect by accentuating something impersonal. On the other hand, the personal abounds in Titus 3:4-7: God acts upon us. Seven times reference is made to the community of we/us. God is seen as a personal Trinity of God, Jesus Christ our Savior, and the Holy Spirit. "A Litany" accentuated one part of the salvation event, marshaling more than twenty-five percent of its words (seventeen out of sixty-three) to create the theme of tears shed for sins committed. Titus 3:4-7 also underlines one part of the salvation event, namely, baptism as the "bath of rebirth and renewal effected by the Holy Spirit." After this illustrative comparison of Titus 3:4-7 with "A Litany," we turn to Titus 3:4-7 within its immediate and broader contexts.

B. THE CONTEXT

In my earlier consideration of Barth's eleventh criteria for determining whether a passage interrupts its context, I gave some explanation of how Titus 3:4-7 relates to its *immediate context*. One further word will suffice here. Titus 3:3 spells out what we were *then* whereas Titus 3:4-7 expresses what we are *now* because of God's action for us. Interested readers might want to note that Ephesians 2:11-13 contains another Pauline example of the frequent New Testament schema of then-now. More about that usage may be found in the chapter on the hymn of Ephesians 2:14-16.

Regarding the *broader context* of Titus 3:4-7 I highlight two points. First, this hymn is the fifth and final trustworthy saying of the Pastoral Epistles. The other four trustworthy sayings are found in 1 Timothy 1:15; 3:1; 4:9 and 2 Timothy 2:11. 2 Timothy 2:11 is very similar to our passage, for it, too, signals a hymn as trustworthy. By denoting a saying as trustworthy, the author indicates that it issues from a collection of hymns or creeds which are to be believed. And since this collection circulated in a Pauline set of communities, one would expect that some of these traditional materials would bear the imprint of Paul's thought. And our expectations are not disappointed. Thus, Paul's thought becomes another context for our study.

From Romans and Galatians especially, we realize that one of Paul's emphases in his discussions with Jewish Christians was that no one is saved by works of the Law. Christians are saved by God's free gift of justification and by faith. (See Rom 3:28: "For we consider that a person is justified by faith apart from works of the Law" [see also Gal 2:15].) With this context of Paul's central theological accent in mind, we can appreciate how the traditional hymn in our passage is Pauline. See especially 3:5, ". . . not because of any righteous deeds which we had done," and 3:7, ". . . so that we, having been made righteous by his grace. . . ."

The second facet of the *broader context* which merits a brief comment here is the polemical situation addressed by all three of the Pastoral Epistles. In this situation the author, writing toward the end of the first century, strives to preserve the Pauline tradition against those who would maintain that creation and institutions like marriage are not good. In such a situation the author wants his readers to show their neighbors, through their good deeds, how beneficial to society Christian faith is. See, e.g., the author's admonition to Titus: "Urge the younger men, similarly, to control themselves, showing yourself as a model of good deeds in every respect, with integrity in your teaching, dignity, and sound speech that cannot be criticized, so that the opponent will be put to shame without anything bad to say about us" (Titus 2:6-8). The interested reader can find more information about this dimension of the broader context of Titus 3:4-7 by consulting my chapters on the hymns of 1 Timothy 3:16 and 2 Timothy 2:11-13.

C. KEY CONCEPTS AND IMAGES

Allow me to underscore the key concepts and images of Titus 3:4-7 by proceeding verse by verse.

Titus 3:4-5a is the introduction to the main clause of the hymn and contains three themes. First, saviors in antiquity were known for their "kindness" and "generous love." As a matter of fact, they were known to be saviors because they manifested such kindness and generosity to people in political, social, or economic need. And it was the duty of those who received the benefactions of the savior to express gratitude to their savior. In a real sense, this hymn is a hymn of gratitude for kindnesses received from our Savior God. Before we leave this notion of savior, I call your attention to the fact that the hymn in verse six calls Jesus Christ "our Savior." What was earlier predicated of God is now said of Jesus. Frederick Danker puts the matter well when he observes: "The attribution of *soter* (savior) to Jesus Christ in the passages just cited (e.g., 2 Tim 1:10; Titus 1:4 and 3:6) does not, then, convey primarily a metaphysical concept but expresses Jesus' function as deliverer. His uniqueness derives from his functional relationship to the unique ancestral God of Israel. Hence the qualifier *Christos* (Christ) . . . the ancestral God of Israel . . . is the Chief Benefactor, whose fundamental expression of concern for humanity is patent in Jesus Christ, the Great Benefactor" (1982, 325).

Second, when we ask the question of *when* God's beneficence for us appeared, the hymn gives us no specific answer. One possible answer is to be found in the salvation conveyed through baptism (3:5). Another possible answer is to be found in the instrumental phrase of 3:6: "through Jesus Christ our savior." Once again we encounter a characteristic of hymns: they tell the truth, but not the entire truth. I refer you to the hymn or creed of Titus 2:11-14 for another allusive answer to our question of when exactly God's beneficence appeared.

My third point, which concerns the hymn's introduction to its principal theme of baptism, is this: the hymn underscores the absolute gratuity of God's saving activity. There is no way that we human beings could justify our situation with God, that is, do what is right/righteous in God's eyes. To use a contemporary example, in my word processing program it is easy to effect justification. I can hit a couple of keys or click my mouse twice and quickly justify the right or left margins of the page I am writing, thus creating order where there was once disarray. But in the process of getting myself saved, I never earn or merit salvation. Salvation is always a gift from the merciful God. No clicking of mice or other wonders of technological gadgetry will justify us before God.

I make a number of points about *Titus 3:5b*, which is the main clause of our hymn: "he saved us through the bath of rebirth and renewal effected by the Holy Spirit." First, "baptism" is such a dominant image in our everyday Christian speech that we can miss the point that our hymn talks about "a bath" (Greek: *loutron*). This image stems from the ubiquitous Roman institution of the public baths, which generally had a central courtyard, changing room, hot bath, steam bath, warm bath, and cold bath. There were baths for men and for women. At their most gracious expression these common baths had lecture halls, elaborate gymnasia, shops, gardens, libraries, and art galleries. Business deals were struck here. People enjoyed and refreshed themselves. And of course, they cleansed themselves. For those who like archaeology, I point out that tourists to Rome flock to see the remains of the immense baths of Caracalla. Tourists to Israel marvel at the sumptuous baths Herod the Great built at his impregnable hilltop fortress at Masada where water was so scarce.

The hymn draws upon images of rebirth and renewal which were popular and powerful in antiquity for expressing what the experience of being saved was like. Most of us are familiar with the image of "rebirth" from John 3:3-5. Allow me to broaden our appreciation of how men and women of the first century C.E. yearned for this rebirth by quoting from the Hermetic literature whose traditions deal with revelations of Thrice-Greatest Hermes and date from the same time as Titus. In the treatise on "Rebirth" there is a dialogue between Trismegistus and a disciple:

> O Trismegistus, I do not know from what kind of womb a man is (re)born, of what kind of seed.
> My child, it is intellectual Wisdom in Silence, and the seed is the true Good.
> Who provides the seed, father? I am altogether at a loss.
> The will of God, my child.
> And what sort of being is he that is begotten, father? For he has no share of the substance that is in me.
> He who is begotten will be another person, God the child of God, the All in All, composed of all the Powers.
> You are telling me a riddle, father, and not speaking as a father to his son.
> This kind of thing, my child, is not taught, but when it is his will God brings it to remembrance (Barrett 1989, 102–3).

Commentators are quick to point out how different the "rebirth" spoken of in Titus 3:5 is from that of the Hermetic literature and the mystery cults which also promised "rebirth." First, Titus 3:5 does not promise some type of ecstasy by which one is momentarily removed from life, but the lasting power of a new life in community. Second, and more importantly, rebirth is not the possession of an elite, but that of all Christians—women and men, slave and free, Gentile and Jew (Dibelius and Conzelmann 1972, 150).

To me the key to how the images of rebirth and renewal function in our hymn is found in the phrase "effected by the Holy Spirit." Ezekiel 37:1-14 witnesses to God's power to breathe new life into the dead and dry bones of Israel. Joel 3:1-2 foretells of a time when God will pour God's Spirit upon all humanity (see Acts 2 for narrative detail on the fulfillment of this promise). In Romans 8:11, Paul spells out the dimensions of new life through God's Spirit: "If the Spirit of the one who raised Jesus from the dead dwells in you, the one who raised Christ from the dead will give life to your mortal bodies also, through his Spirit that dwells in you." And in Romans 12:2, Paul talks about the renewal which God has effected in the Christians' minds, so that they can know God's will and do it. Put in other words, what the bath does to the outside of the believer relates symbolically to what actually occurs inside the believer: the Spirit effects purification and revitalization and renewal in the ethical realm. And there is more: as Paul says in 2 Corinthians 1:22—and as this hymn says in its final verse—the Spirit is the first installment of what is to come.

So from what has God saved us by means of the bath? Put negatively, God has saved us from not being born again, from not being renewed. God has rescued us from the sad ethical mess bemoaned in Titus 3:3. Put positively, God has given us new life among fellow believers, who also have undergone the public bath of God our Savior, Savior Jesus Christ, and Holy Spirit.

Two points call for attention in Titus 3:6-7, the concluding verses of our hymn. First, the abundance of God's Spirit has come about because of the action of "Jesus Christ our savior." If we stick within the Pauline tradition, 1 Corinthians 15:45 provides us with the background for the thought in our hymn: the risen Lord Jesus has become a life-giving Spirit. That is, Jesus, crucified and risen, is the giver of God's Spirit.

Second, although the earlier parts of the hymn gave full voice to the refrain that we are saved, verse seven stops that refrain in midbreath with its version of what has been called the Pauline eschatological reserve. That is, we are not yet saved, for we are heirs *in hope* of the fullness of God's salvation. Perhaps, we can see how deeply our hymn is indebted to the Pauline tradition by quoting Romans 8:23-24: ". . . but we ourselves, who have the firstfruits of the Spirit, we also groan within ourselves as we wait for adoption, the redemption of our bodies. For in hope we were saved."

In my analysis of the key concepts and images of Titus 3:4-7, I have given pride of place to the "bath of rebirth." But at the same time we should not lose sight of the hymn's joyous confession that we are recipients of the kindness and generous love of our Savior God, Holy Spirit, and Savior Jesus Christ. All praise to our Triune God!

D. Reflection Starters

My first thought centers on the Pauline theme which pervades our hymn: *God's salvation is an utterly free gift.* Left unsaid in our hymn is how much we need God's gift of rescue. The hymn puts Savior God, Savior Jesus Christ, and lavishly-bestowed Holy Spirit in the foreground. Gratitude is our fitting response to such an extraordinary present gift which has eternal consequences for the future.

Second, I suggest that reflection upon Titus 3:4-7 can help us deepen our *understanding of the Holy Spirit.* Many contemporary Pauline reflections upon the Holy Spirit have drawn their inspiration from 1 Corinthians 12-14, where Paul discusses the various charisms given to women and men in the Christian community. The thought behind mention of the Holy Spirit in our hymn is not 1 Corinthians 12–14, but Romans 8. In Romans the Holy Spirit is the divine agent of our revitalization and renewal and is the down payment of God's future gifts. It is the gift of God's Spirit in us believers that prompts us as children to utter "Abba, that is, Father" (Rom 8:15) and that enkindles in us hope of eternal life.

On another level and through the imagery of rebirth, the Spirit is likened to a woman bringing forth new life through childbirth, as is also the case in John 3:3-6. As Elizabeth A. Johnson reminds us: "In (early) Syriac Christianity the Spirit's image was consistently that of the brooding or hovering mother bird. Among other maternal activities, the Spirit mothers Jesus into life at his conception in Mary's womb, empowers him into mission at his baptism, and brings believers to birth out of the watery womb of the baptismal font" (1992, 86). Perhaps it is time to use Titus 3:4-7 as a means of retrieving this powerful image of creative love, tenderness, nurture, warmth, and protection for our catechesis on the Spirit's role in the salvific bath.

Third, it may be that we can draw a lesson or two from *contexts.* Recall how the author of the Pastoral Epistles contextualized the hymn of Titus 3:4-7 by connecting it with verse eight: because God has been so beneficent to us, let's engage in beneficence to others through our good deeds. Then again there's the very warm and welcoming context of the Christmas Mass at Dawn which spotlights the opening verse of our hymn so much that its reference to the salvific bath remains in darkness. This context proclaims more loudly, it seems, than church bells that "the kindness and generous love of God our savior appeared" in Jesus' birth in Bethlehem.

During recent classroom discussions of Titus 3:4-7 my students and I began to discern more clearly the *communal nature* of the bath. My fourth reflection is a digest of our communal discernment. The Roman institution of the common bath, from which the composer of Titus 3:4-7 draws his imagery, has at least two key dimensions. One is the dimension of personal bathing and refreshment, which is readily captured in our frequent North American experience of being rejuvenated or revitalized or having all life's cares washed away by a hot bath or shower. The other dimension is social or communal, as we realize that the Roman bath was the center of communal life. The following contemporary experiences may provide analogies which will help us retrieve the communal nature of the bath. One analogy is the health club. Then there are family and social outings to the lake or beach, or trips with family and friends to hot springs. In these analogies, which could be multiplied, the aspect of private bathing is in the background. In the foreground is the public and social dimension. In conclusion, the initiatory bath is once and for all and is deeply private and personal, but the communal dimension of that bath beckons us to return time and again to be with the community of those bathed by our Triune God.

I conclude with an observation which applies to all our attempts to bring into our daily lives the message of the hymns we encounter in the New Testament. Recently, while on fraternal visitation in Toronto, Canada, I went for a walk and noticed a billboard with the command in huge letters, REUPHOLSTER YOUR HEAD! Since the hairs on my head are easily numbered, I was immediately interested in the full message on the billboard. In smaller letters the billboard had: Hats from $1. I laughed, and since I was working on Titus 3:4-7 at that time, I laughed even more heartily. Would that we could renew our head with its self-centered interests as easily as we can don a new chapeau! But perhaps that is the wrong thought and borders on "righteousness by works." Renewal is a gift and is just as free as the life given by the mothering Spirit. Thanks be to God for the gift of this Spirit who forms us into the women and men of the community of "the bathed."

ANNOTATED BIBLIOGRAPHY

Barrett, C. K. *The New Testament Background: Selected Documents.* Rev. ed. San Francisco: HarperSanFrancisco, 1989. This very handy volume with introductions and notes by a leading New Testament scholar devotes pp. 93–103 to documents purporting to contain the revelations of the god, Hermes.

Barth, Markus. *Ephesians: Introduction, Translation, and Commentary on Chapters 1–3.* Anchor Bible 34A. Garden City: Doubleday, 1974. In my opinion Titus 3:4-7 fails to meet the following five criteria listed by Barth on pp. 6-8. Titus 3:4-7 lacks a special conjunction like "as" or "therefore" at its beginning or ending (criterion no. 1). Titus 3:4-7 does not begin with a simple relative pronoun "who" or in "whom" as is the case with 1 Timothy 3:16 or Colossians 1:15-20 (criterion no. 2). Titus 3:4-7 does not fit criterion no. 5: "A concern for brevity is reflected by the omission of the article before key terms (1 Tim 3:16). But this interest yields often to that of precision or pleonasm which finds its expression in synonyms, genitive appositions, baroque repetitions (Eph 1:4-14)" (7). Surely, Titus 3:4-7 cannot "easily and naturally be divided into cola, lines of similar or equal length which contain a consistent number of beats, perhaps of syllables, too" (criterion no. 7, p. 7). Finally, nowhere does Titus 3:4-7 emphasize "the cosmic extension of God's or Christ's role" as in Colossians 1:15-20 (criterion no. 10, p. 8).

Danker, Frederick W. *Benefactor: Epigraphic Study of a Graeco-Roman and New Testament Semantic Field.* St. Louis: Clayton Publishing House, 1982. An excellent collection of materials on an understudied motif. Because of its brevity and importance for interpreting Titus 3:4-7 I quote the 48 B.C.E. decree by Asians in honor of Julius Caesar: "The cities in Asia and the [townships] and the tribal districts honor Gaius Julius Caesar, son of Gaius, Pontifex, Imperator, and Consul for the second time, descendant of Ares and Aphrodite, our God Manifest and Common Savior of all human life" (pp. 213–14).

Dibelius, Martin, and Hans Conzelmann. *The Pastoral Epistles: A Commentary on the Pastoral Epistles.* Hermeneia Commentary Series. Philadelphia: Fortress, 1972. A learned and concise commentary with abundant and helpful references to non-Old Testament backgrounds.

Johnson, Elizabeth A. *She Who Is: The Mystery of God in Feminist Theological Discourse.* New York: Crossroad, 1992. An excellent book on "theo-logy."

Quinn, Jerome D. *The Letter to Titus: A New Translation with Notes and Commentary and An Introduction to Titus, I and II Timothy, The Pastoral Epistles.* Anchor Bible 35. New York: Doubleday, 1990. A comprehensive commentary. Quinn is of the opinion that while Titus 3:4-7 has hymnic elements, it is not a hymn.

N.B. The interested reader will find additional bibliography on the Pastoral Epistles at the end of my chapters on 1 Timothy 3:16 and 2 Timothy 2:11-13.

VII-2. 1 Peter 3:18-22—
Christ Jesus, the Fallen Angels, and Salvific Baptism

A. TRANSLATION AND STRUCTURAL ANALYSIS

3:18a *For Christ also suffered for sins once,*
3:18b *the righteous for the sake of the unrighteous,*
3:18c *that he might lead you to God.*
3:18d *Put to death in the flesh,*
3:18e *he was brought to life in the spirit.*
3:19 In it he also went to preach to the spirits in prison,
3:20 who had once been disobedient while God patiently waited in the days of Noah during the building of the ark, in which a few persons, eight in all, were saved through water.
3:21 This prefigured baptism, which saves you now. It is not a removal of dirt from the body, but an appeal to God for a clear conscience, through the resurrection of Jesus Christ,
3:22 *who is at the right hand of God, having gone into heaven, with angels, authorities, and powers subject to him* (NAB adapted).

In what follows I will provide a road map through the thick forest of traditions which constitute 1 Peter 3:18-22. In the section on key concepts and images I will give more detail on the meaning of the individual traditions.

Scholars commonly maintain that 1 Peter 3:18 and 3:22 contain hymnic formulations and that a primitive baptismal catechesis lies behind 1 Peter 3:19-21, which is written in prose. In the translation, I italicized verses eighteen and twenty-two to highlight them. If these verses are read together, they provide a chronological summary of the events of salvation: Christ's death to wipe away sin for us, Christ's resurrection, and Christ's ascension to heaven with its accompaniments of sitting at God's right hand and having all evil powers subject to him. The key elements of this very early hymn/creed might be translated as follows:

"PuT to death in the flesh" (3:18)
"broughT to life in the spirit" (3:18)
"wenT into heaven" (3:22)

The following observations spell out the hymnic form of these clauses. Each clause begins with a Greek verb, which ends in *theis*. I have tried to capture this Greek artistic touch by capitalizing the final *t* on the endings of the English verbs. Another poetic nicety occurs in the contrast between "put to death in the flesh" and "brought to life in the spirit," a contrast enhanced by a Greek construction *(men . . . de),* which might be translated "on the one hand . . . on the other hand," but is best left untranslated in this instance. Further, the sequence is chronological and soteriological—death/resurrection/ascension—and provides a summary of the kerygma.

To the core hymn/creed of 3:18de and 3:22 the author of 1 Peter has added 3:18a-c as an introduction, which links all of 3:18d-22 to what preceded it. This introduction consists largely of traditional material about the saving significance of Jesus' death. Another important addition is the catechetical tradition of 3:19-21, which is the only place in 1 Peter where the author talks explicitly about baptism. Verse twenty-two rounds off our passage by quoting traditions about Christ's exaltation.

A close scrutiny of our passage reveals that there is a certain amount of redundancy. Some commentators argue that this redundancy is proof that the author has taken over various traditions from different thought worlds and not harmonized them. I belong to the camp which sees in these duplications the author's artistic hand. First, the author presents three different, but complementary, views of Jesus' death in 3:18a-d: Christ suffered for sins once (3:18a); that he might lead you to God (3:18c); he was put to death in the flesh (3:18d). Then the author develops a short chiastic or cross-like structure in 3:18e-22:

resurrection (he was brought to life in the spirit—3:18e)
ascension (preaching to the imprisoned spirits—3:19)
resurrection (through the resurrection of Christ—3:21)
ascension (all of 3:22)

Thus, if resurrection is *A* and ascension is *B,* we end up with the chiastic pattern of *ABAB.* And in the midst of this pattern is the tradition about baptism. If this tradition is denoted as *C,* then the complete pattern is *ABCAB.* Lest my readers think that I love to play the scholarly and meaningless game of finding chiasms behind almost every hymnic passage in the New Testament, let me point out the theological significance of the author's chiastic structure. In my view the purpose of the author's chiasm is to develop a cosmic theology of baptism. That is, the author has placed baptism *(C)* in the center, so that it might be interpreted by the salvific events in *ABAB,* to wit, the baptized share in Jesus' conquest of the disobedient and imprisoned evil spirits through his death, resurrection, and ascension.

Having provided you with a quick tour of the dense forest of traditions in 1 Peter 3:18-22, I now proceed to offer insights into these various traditions and how they mutually interpret one another. The interested reader might want to refer back to Chapter II for more detail about the close relationship between creed and hymn.

B. The Context

The immediate and broader contexts of 1 Peter 3:18-22 can be treated together. 1 Peter was written around 80 C.E. to encourage its Gentile Christian readers to persevere in their faith in a situation of largely verbal harassment. A glimpse of this purpose can be seen in 3:15-17: "Always be ready to give an explanation to anyone who asks you for a reason for your hope, but do it with gentleness and reverence, keeping your conscience clear, so that, when *you are maligned, those who defame your good conduct in Christ* may themselves be put to shame. For it is better to suffer for doing good, if that be the will of God, than for doing evil" (emphasis mine).

As we shall see shortly, another very important context for our passage stems from Christian and Jewish reflections upon and traditions about the significance of Enoch and Noah, which lie behind what the author says in 3:19-20.

C. KEY CONCEPTS AND IMAGES

In order to appreciate fully the richness of this passage, we will discuss its key concepts and images as we move systematically through each verse.

In the Old Testament background, which pulsates beneath the surface of *1 Peter 3:18a-c,* is the viewpoint that women and men have sinned against God and need to be set right with God and to find atonement for their sins. The sacrificial system of the Old Testament made atonement with God possible on a regular basis by the shedding of the blood of animals. But the Prophet Isaiah foresaw a day when the suffering of one person, the Suffering Servant, would free people from their sins. Isaiah 53:5 reads: "But he was pierced for our offenses, crushed for our sins. Upon him was the chastisement that makes us whole, by his stripes we were healed." 53:11 goes on to say: "Because of his affliction he shall see the light in fullness of days. Through his suffering, my servant shall justify men and women, and their guilt he shall bear."

Drawing heavily upon Isaiah's Suffering Servant imagery, our author and the tradition before him proclaim that Christ died once and for all and canceled the sins which separated us from God and made us liable to God's judgment. In proclaiming this saving reality, our author joins hands with those formulators of the traditions behind 1 Corinthians 15:3 ("Christ died for our sins"), Galatians 1:4 ("who gave himself for our sins"), and Hebrews 10:12 ("But this one offered one sacrifice for sins, and took his seat forever at the right hand of God"). Jesus, the Righteous One, and not the blood of holocausts, has liberated the unrighteous from their sins and from the effects of their sins—guilt and alienation from God—by shedding his blood on the cross.

Our author makes a final point about the effect of Jesus' death: ". . . that he might lead you to God." On one level, the author underscores the fact that believers now have confident access to

God, who will hear their cries for help. On another level, the author maintains that just as Christ went through suffering to God, so too will he lead his followers through suffering to God.

The hymnic and creedal affirmation, "put to death in the flesh, he was brought to life in the spirit" of *1 Peter 3:18de,* has echoes in other New Testament letters. Quoting earlier tradition, Paul writes to the Romans concerning "the gospel about God's Son, descended from David according to the *flesh,* but established as Son of God in power according to the *spirit* of holiness through resurrection from the dead, Jesus Christ our Lord" (1:3-4). And 1 Timothy 3:16 quotes an early hymn about Jesus Christ "who was manifested in the *flesh,* vindicated in the *spirit.*"

What 1 Peter 3:18de (and its New Testament companions) says is multiple. Jesus was indeed a complete human being. And as such he died, just as all human beings do. As "put to death" indicates, Jesus died at the hands of others—a reference to his crucifixion. Thus, the author expands upon the previous two meanings he gave to Jesus' death (to take sins away; to lead us to God) and introduces a third view of the meaning of Jesus' death.

But Jesus' death was not the end of his life or its meaning for humankind, for "he was brought to life in the spirit." From studies of Old Testament and New Testament anthropology, it is clear that our author is not using "flesh" to talk about Jesus' body and "spirit" to talk about his soul. He is talking about humanity from the vantage point of two modes of existence. Jesus participated in the weaknesses, limitations, sufferings, temptations, and death which befall all human beings. That is what "flesh" means. But Jesus is now in the mode of the spirit, that is, his weaknesses and limitations are cast aside through the power, which is God's Spirit. To all appearances he was rejected by God in his sufferings and death, but now he has been vindicated by the life of God's Spirit. God has replaced death by the life of the Spirit. In brief, God has raised Jesus from the dead.

Perhaps, the following example will enable us to catch some glimmer of the mystery which our text seeks to express. In the Eucharistic chapel of the Shrine of Our Lady of Guadalupe in Mexico City, there is a gigantic mural of the risen Christ. Jesus, identifiably human, is clad in a flowing white sheet and holds a flimsy cross in his hand. He seems to be galloping forth from the tomb, the place of death, his face suffused with the spirit of joy, taking giant steps into life, heading back to women and men to tell them the good news of what God has done for them in him and to offer them a share in his new life in the Spirit.

1 Peter 3:18a–c tells us in two different ways about the effects of Jesus' death: it has canceled sins and it has opened up heaven for us. And 1 Peter 3:18de tells us that the fully human Jesus was put to death. But that was not the final word, for God raised Jesus and gave him new life in the Spirit. At the end of 1 Peter 3:21, when the author is completing his catechesis on baptism, he will again refer to Jesus' resurrection. The effects of baptism are the result of Jesus' sharing of his life of the Spirit with us. By inserting the teaching of 1 Peter 3:19-21 between two references to God's resurrection of Jesus, the author elaborates on the meaning of Jesus' resurrection for the evil powers of this world (3:19) and for the baptized (3:20-21).

We come now to what many scholars consider the most difficult verse in the entire New Testament, *1 Peter 3:19,* with its message of Jesus' preaching to the spirits in prison. We have become accustomed to read about and benefit from the fresh insights into the Gospels which scholars have derived from new investigations into the social, intellectual, and political backgrounds of the first century of the common era. For example, the discovery of the Dead Sea scrolls in 1946 at Qumran in the Judean desert has benefited scholars of John's Gospel because these scrolls provided evidence of a Jewish, non-Gnostic religious use of the contrast between light and darkness. In a similar way, the rediscovery of the literature about Enoch in the nineteenth century has enhanced interpreters' knowledge of the possible thought background behind 1 Peter 3:19. In what follows I will present some background material on the Old Testament figure, Enoch, which might be unfamiliar to many of you, but will give us a key to unlock the mystery of 1 Peter 3:19, just as reading the Dead Sea scrolls opened the eyes of many to see anew the meaning of the Johannine Jesus' religious language about light and darkness.

The cardinal text for reflections upon Enoch is Genesis 5:24: "Then Enoch walked with God, and he was no longer here, for

God took him." Two New Testament letters refer to Enoch. The Letter to the Hebrews finds in Enoch a prime example of faith: "By faith Enoch was taken up so that he should not see death, and 'he was found no more because God had taken him.' Before he was taken up, he was attested to have pleased God. But without faith it is impossible to please him, for anyone who approaches God must believe that he exists and that he rewards those who seek him" (11:5-6). The Letter of Jude in verses fourteen and fifteen considers the words of Enoch authoritative and quotes him: "Enoch, of the seventh generation from Adam, prophesied also about them when he said, 'Behold, the Lord has come with his countless holy ones to execute judgment on all and to convict everyone for all the godless deeds that they committed and for all the harsh words godless sinners have uttered against him'" (the reference is to the highly influential, but pseudepigraphical 1 Enoch 1:9).

The reverence which the New Testament authors of Hebrews and Jude had for Enoch is paralleled in certain Jewish literature, especially the books of First and Second Enoch, which are dated between 200 B.C.E. and 100 C.E. For our purposes three observations are important. First, the books of Enoch contain the divine revelations which Enoch saw and heard during his journeys through the various heavens. Second, these books, especially 1 Enoch 6–16, reflect upon Genesis 6:1-4, which describes the sin of the angels, also called "sons of God" or "Watchers," who disobediently abandoned their place in heaven to take human wives to themselves and taught humankind all kinds of evils, e.g., magic, oppression, war. According to 1 Enoch, this sin of the fallen angels was equivalent to the original sin of Adam and Eve. Third, for their sin of disobedience these angels are imprisoned—either forever or until God's final judgment upon them. According to 1 Enoch 14:5 their prison is inside the earth. According to 2 Enoch 7:2, Enoch sees the condemned angels in the second heaven. In this connection, it should be recalled that after narrating the sin of these angels in 6:1-4, the Book of Genesis continues by narrating the story of Noah and the flood in chapters six through nine. I round off this excursus into Jewish reflection upon Enoch by calling to mind that the Letter of Jude, verse six is heir to a similar tradition about the disobedient angels: "The angels too, who did not keep to their own domain but deserted their proper dwelling, he has kept in eternal chains, in gloom, for the judgment of the great day."

In summary, Enoch is a unique biblical figure because God took him up to heaven. As a person of faith and the mediator of divine revelation, he was highly regarded by both Christian (Hebrews and Jude) and Jewish (1–2 Enoch) authors. His revelations place the cause of the reign of sin in this world not only with the original sin of Adam and Eve, but also with the original sin of the angels referred to in Genesis 6:1-4. If Jesus Christ is to have any significance in the universe of discourse represented by the Enoch literature, he must deal definitively with the imprisoned evil angels who brought about sin.

The above background on Enoch gives us the password which opens the door to the meaning of 1 Peter 3:19. In his resurrected state of being filled with God's life, Jesus Christ goes to the imprisoned spirits. These "spirits" (Greek: *pneumata*) are the evil spirits described in Genesis 6:1-4 and depicted by the various Christian and Jewish traditions quoted above. Just as "spirit" in 1 Peter 3:18 did not refer to Jesus' soul, so too "spirits" in 3:19 do not refer to the "souls" of human beings. The interpretive parallels for "spirits" are to be found in the Gospels: "When it was evening, they brought him many who were possessed by demons, and he drove out the *spirits* by a word and cured all the sick" (Matt 8:16); "Nevertheless, do not rejoice because the *spirits* are subject to you, but rejoice because your names are written in heaven" (Luke 10:20).

The reference to these spirits being *in prison* seems a clear reference to the story of the fallen angels of Genesis 6:1-4 and their imprisonment by God. To them Jesus Christ *proclaims* that God's reign is indeed present in what God has done in his resurrection and that their power to alienate people from God is destroyed. Put another way, in Jesus Christ God has conquered the power of the original sin brought into the world by the disobedient angels. In 1 Peter 3:22 the author will express a part of this theological truth in a different way and will use different terminology to describe these malevolent powers: ". . . with angels, authorities, and powers subject to Jesus Christ." If the cosmic meaning of 1 Peter 3:19 is to make sense to us, we may have to forget about the dominant Pauline imagery of Jesus as the New Adam who has conquered the original sin of the old Adam and into whose death and resurrection Christians are baptized (Romans 5–6). 1 Peter 3:18-22 presents a quite different view of Jesus Christ and of baptism.

A sampling of New Testament thought about Noah and his times will help us appreciate what our author says in *1 Peter 3:20*. The author of 2 Peter cites what God did to the angels of Genesis 6:1-4, to the contemporaries of Noah, and to Lot's contemporaries in Sodom and Gomorrah, to make his point that God punishes the unrighteous and preserves the righteous. In 2 Peter 2:4-5, the author deals specifically with the angels and Noah: "For if God did not spare the angels when they sinned, but condemned them to the chains of Tartarus and handed them over to be kept for judgment; and if he did not spare the ancient world, even though he preserved Noah, a herald of righteousness, together with seven others, when he brought a flood upon the godless world. . . ." From 2 Peter we again learn the magnitude of the sin of the angels and see how the author singles out Noah as a preacher of righteousness.

The author of Hebrews has this to say of Noah: "By faith Noah, warned about what was not yet seen, with reverence built an ark for the salvation of his household. Through this he condemned the world and inherited the righteousness that comes through faith" (11:7). As is his wont in chapter eleven, the author of Hebrews finds in the biblical hero Noah an epitome of faith.

Finally, I quote from Jesus' words in Luke 17:26-27: "As it was in the days of Noah, so it will be in the days of the Son of Man; they were eating and drinking, marrying and giving in marriage up to the day that Noah entered the ark, and the flood came and destroyed them all." The moral denseness and indifference of Noah's contemporaries are almost proverbial here.

The three New Testament passages cited above surely help us understand the figure of faith-filled and righteous Noah, but the sequence of thought between "disobedient angels in prison" and the mention of Noah needs further clarification. This clarification comes from the account of the flood in Genesis 6–9, which connects the sin of the fallen angels with the human sins against which God reacted by punishing humankind with the Flood. The "while" of our translation of 1 Peter 3:20 should not be pressed literalistically, as if the disobedience of the fallen angels was contemporaneous with the Flood. Their disobedience was 120 years before the Flood, but the effects of their primal sin were corrupting men and women all during that time while God was patient. The author uses biblical shorthand, telescopes time, and brings together the primal sin of the angels and the Flood. The author concludes 1 Peter 3:20 by mentioning that eight were saved through water. This conclusion leads him into verse twenty-one, which contains the heart of his explicit teaching about baptism.

Our author begins 1 Peter 3:21 with ". . . this prefigured baptism, which saves you now." It is clear that "this" is an explicit reference to "the water" of the flood. But before exploring in some detail the obvious point of comparing the water of the flood with Christian baptism, I want to point out some other reasons why the author quoted this baptismal catechesis here. First, just as the addressees of 1 Peter are suffering from the indifference of their fellow citizens, so too were Noah and his family. Second, smallness of numbers should not discourage the addressees of 1 Peter, for only eight were saved during Noah's time. Third, God is patient with those who scoff at the conduct of believers just as God was patient as Noah built the ark. Fourth, and most important, the readers of 1 Peter should be buoyed up by the faith and perseverance of Noah, who trusted in God's word although he had nothing concrete on which to base his trust.

Our author agrees with the traditional baptismal catechesis which he quotes and which states that the saving water of the flood prefigures salvific baptism. Our attempts to clarify our author's statement will have to contend with two factors. First, this is the only reference in the entire New Testament to the truth that baptism itself saves. Second, we will need an alternative translation of verse twenty-one to appreciate the refinement of the author's thought. I begin with such a translation and then move into clarifying the author's thought, which might at first blush give the impression that the mere ritual of baptism saves. I translate 3:21 as follows:

> Baptism now saves you,
> which is not the removal of the dirt of the flesh,

> but it is an appeal to God for a good conscience,
> through the resurrection of Jesus Christ.

In my translation and in my spatial separation of the clauses I have tried to emphasize a number of points. First, it is through the power of God's Spirit active in the risen Jesus Christ that baptism saves. It is the risen Jesus Christ, as 1 Peter 3:18-19 explained, who enjoys freedom from the bonds of death and corruption and who has proclaimed his victory over the evil spirits and their power to cause men and women to rebel against God. Just as God saved Noah and his family from physical death through water, so too does God save through the water of baptism the Christian from spiritual death and from submission to the evils unleashed in this world by the primal sin of the fallen angels of Genesis 6:1-4. But there is a new element in this comparison. For *now* God saves through the power of Jesus Christ. Surely, this baptismal teaching is not Paul's teaching of being baptized into Christ's death (Romans 6), though it, too, powerfully accentuates, as does Paul, the truth that God, and no amount of human willing, saves through Jesus Christ.

But the divine component of salvific baptism is not the only one highlighted by our author and the tradition quoted. In the middle clauses of our translation the author wrestles to explain the human contribution to salvific baptism. By saying that baptism is not the removal of the dirt of the flesh, our author separates baptism from the ritual cleansings found in almost all religions. He also sharply distinguishes baptism from the human endeavors to remove the dirt of sin which humans generate in their weakness and propensity to sin (the meaning of "flesh" here).

If baptism is understood as such, then wherein is its human component? In the translation I have adopted, the human component consists in the (sincere) appeal or pledge of the (repentant) human being to God for a clear or clean conscience. Behind this translation there are three subcomponents: (1) a profound trust that God will forgive sins which stand in the way of a person having a clear conscience; (2) closely aligned to this, an appreciation that salvific baptism is God's free gift (grace); and (3) the human resolve to live such a life as to retain a clear conscience.

I stand in awe at the profound understandings of baptism and of Jesus Christ which course through the baptismal catechesis of 1 Peter 3:19-21 and at how the Christians in the first decades of Christianity interpreted their experience on the basis of the Old Testament and their experience of salvation. In the final verse of this theological and Christological masterpiece, we will be invited to praise our Lord Jesus Christ, to whom are subject all evil powers which might separate us baptized from our Lord.

In 1 Peter 3:22 our author concludes the chiastic or cross-like structure he commenced in 3:18: resurrection-ascension-baptism-resurrection-ascension. He still has in view the saving effects of baptism. The risen Jesus Christ, who saves the baptized through giving them the life of his Spirit, now occupies the position of power at God's right hand, having ascended into heaven, and is conqueror of all the evil powers. In professing these truths about Jesus Christ, the author builds upon various traditions. It is unfortunate that both the NAB and the NRSV sacrifice the author's artistic and profoundly theological use of tradition on the altar of achieving the smooth reading of a chronological sequence: went into heaven, is seated, etc. In my translation I follow the Greek sequence: "who is at the right hand of God, having gone into heaven, with angels, authorities, and powers subject to him."

As we saw earlier, the author has as his hymnic and creedal centerpiece: put to death in the flesh, brought to life in the spirit, has gone into heaven. The final element, "has gone into heaven," occurs in 1 Peter 3:22 and is sandwiched between and thereby interpreted by two other traditional formulations. In other words, the risen Jesus Christ has gone into heaven to assume the powerful position of being seated at God's right hand and to subject to himself all evil powers. Although they employ different universes of thought, these two traditions say much the same as what is said in 1 Peter 3:19: Jesus preached to the fallen angels in prison that God's reign has conquered their power. In 3:22, however, it is made very clear that the risen Jesus Christ exercises God's power over all evil forces as God's right-hand authority. I will round off our discussion by citing some of the evidence for my contention that two other traditions bracket "has gone into heaven" in 3:22.

The best evidence for the tradition in 3:22 that Jesus "is seated at God's right hand," is the creedal formulation which Paul incorporates into his thought in Romans 8:34: ". . . Christ Jesus, who died, rather, was raised, who also is at the right hand of God, who indeed intercedes for us." Both Paul and our author borrow tradition from the Christians who preceded them.

References to angels, authorities, and powers abound in the Pauline letters, especially Colossians and Ephesians. Particularly illustrative for our purposes is the tradition incorporated into Ephesians 1:20-21 which speaks of the power God "worked in Christ, raising him from the dead and seating him at his right hand in the heavens, far above every principality, authority, power, and dominion, and every name that is named not only in this age but also in the one to come." 1 Peter 3:22 and similar traditions about the subjection of the evil powers to Jesus Christ put into graphic language Jesus' cosmic and universal rule. There is nothing and no one who is not subject to him. Not even those disobedient angels mentioned in Genesis 6:1-4, whose sin caused the human race so much grief. Hurrah! Alleluia!

In summary, through its use of various traditions 1 Peter 3:18-22 sings loudly of the saving power of Jesus' death, resurrection, ascension into heaven, and conquest of the evil powers and of a baptism received in trust and with a clear conscience.

D. REFLECTION STARTERS

In my first reflection I plead for acceptance of the *unique view of Jesus Christ and baptism* expressed in 1 Peter 3:18-22. One of the beauties of the New Testament is that it provides a stage for many different voices to sing the praises of what God has accomplished for believers in Jesus Christ. The most familiar voice in the New Testament is that of Paul, whose rich bass has inspired generations of Christians with his rendition of the themes of Christ the New Adam and of baptism into Christ's death. As a matter of fact, Paul's rendition of these mysteries has stolen the show with the result that listeners do not pack the house to hear other renditions of the themes of salvation and of baptism. But 1 Peter 3:18-22 is one of those unfamiliar renditions which begs for an appreciative audience.

Behind the thought of 1 Peter 3:18-22 is an effort to relate Jesus soteriologically to the pervasive power of evil in the world. All evil powers are subject to the risen Jesus Christ (3:22), who has also vanquished the evil angels who helped introduce sin into the world in the first place (3:19). Put another way, the risen Jesus Christ has removed the definitive effect of this original sin and shares this blessing in baptism. This strange view of Jesus' proclamation of victory to the imprisoned evil angels is kept alive today by the Ethiopian Christian Church, whose teachings, like those of a number of early Church Fathers, were influenced by the revelations of Enoch. Perhaps, we have much to learn from them in this ecumenical age.

Second, this passage accords well with the author's purpose of *providing encouragement* to his harassed addressees. From the baptismal catechesis of 1 Peter 3:18-22 they learned afresh that their baptismal salvation was effected by the power of the risen Jesus Christ who will not allow anything, especially persecution, to separate his beloved people from him. The assurance that the author gives to his addressees might well boost the morale of those of us who live in what is daily becoming a post-Christian society. We are more becoming the few, whose conduct should raise question marks in the minds of our neighbors and fellow workers. In this context, we can learn from Dorothy Day, cofounder of the Catholic Worker Movement, who found particular solace in 1 Peter 3:15 when she was criticized for what we today would call her countercultural "preferential option for the poor." 1 Peter 3:15 reads: "Always be ready to give an explanation to anyone who asks you for a reason for your hope."

A third reflection issues from *a universalist reading* of the ambiguous 1 Peter 3:19. I refer readers who are interested in more detail about ambiguity in poetry and hymns to the chapter on Ephesians 2:14-16. In my comments above on 1 Peter 3:19, I have provided my readers with what I consider the probable reading. I advise you that other scholars, e.g., Goppelt and Perkins, see in 1 Peter 3:19 a possible reference to Jesus' preaching of salvation to the unrepentant sinners of Noah's time, whose souls/spirits are now imprisoned. In this reading, Jesus preaches forgiveness and does so to legendary sinners. This reading, therefore, spotlights the universality of Jesus' salvation. "The cosmic reach of that salvation extends back to beginnings of humankind at the time of the flood" (Perkins 1995, 66). Some would take this reading to mean that the all merciful Jesus Christ gives even the most hardened sinners a second chance.

To conclude, we may be able to see how unique the message of 1 Peter 3:18-22 really is by comparing it with the spiritual "Ride On, King Jesus." In both traditional pieces Jesus Christ is Conqueror. In both, the believer has firm confidence in Jesus as Savior. I would invite you to explore other comparisons between 1 Peter 3:18-22 and this spiritual as a way of consolidating what you have learned in this chapter:

> Ride on, King Jesus, no man can a-hinder me.
>
> For he is King of Kings, He is Lord of Lords.
> Jesus Christ, the first and last,
> No man works like him.
>
> King Jesus rides a milk-white horse,
> No man works like him.
> The river of Jordan he did cross.
> No man works like him.
>
> King Jesus rides in the middle of the air.
> He calls the saints from ev'rywhere.
>
> He is the King, He is the Lord.
> Yes, he is the King, He is the Lord, Ha!
> No man works like him.
>
> Ride on, ride on, ride on, ride on, Jesus!

ANNOTATED BIBLIOGRAPHY

Charlesworth, James H., ed. *The Old Testament Pseudepigrapha*. Vol. 1, *Apocalyptic Literature and Testaments*. Garden City: Doubleday, 1983. This volume contains fresh translations, introductions, and notes on 1 and 2 Enoch by E. Isaac and F. I. Anderson respectively.

Dalton, William Joseph. *Christ's Proclamation to the Spirits: A Study of 1 Peter 3:18–4:6*. 2nd fully rev. ed. Analecta Biblica 23. Rome: Pontificio Instituto Biblico, 1989. The author argues that 1 Peter

3:19 refers to the evil angels of Genesis 6:1-4 and that background for this verse is to be sought in 1 and 2 Enoch. Very scholarly.

Dalton, William Joseph. "The First Epistle of Peter." *New Jerome Biblical Commentary*. Eds. Raymond E. Brown, Joseph A. Fitzmyer, and Roland E. Murphy, 57:1-28. Englewood Cliffs: Prentice Hall, 1990. A shorter, popular presentation of the argument of his dissertation.

Goppelt, Leonhard. *A Commentary on I Peter*. Grand Rapids: Eerdmans, 1993. Translation of a classic German commentary. Author argues that Jesus proclaimed forgiveness to the imprisoned spirits of the sinners of Noah's time.

Marshall, I. Howard. *1 Peter*. The IVP New Testament Commentary Series; Downers Grove: InterVarsity, 1991. Popular and insightful commentary by an internationally recognized New Testament scholar. Basically agrees with Dalton's views.

Michaels, J. Ramsey. *1 Peter*. Word Biblical Commentary 49. Waco: Word Books, 1988. A learned and clearly written commentary, whose views on our passage vary slightly from those of Dalton and Marshall.

Perkins, Pheme. *First and Second Peter, James, and Jude*. Interpretation Series. Louisville: John Knox, 1995. A clearly written and well-researched commentary, which interprets "the spirits" of 1 Peter 3:19 as humans.

VIII. Movement 5

2 Timothy 2:11-13— We Sinners Can Depend on Jesus at the Last Judgment

A. Translation and Structural Analysis

The saying is faithful:
For if we have died with him, we shall also live with him (line 1).
If we remain steadfast, we shall also reign with him (line 2).
If we shall disown him, he will also disown us (line 3).
If we are unfaithful, he remains faithful (line 4).
For he cannot disown himself (line 5) [NAB adapted].

I have adapted the NAB translation to illustrate more clearly the hymnic structure of this "faithful" saying. I have also divided the verses into five lines and assigned a number to each line, so that the hymn might be discussed more easily.

Two observations will underscore the artistry of this hymn. First, this faithful saying consists of a mere twenty-eight words in Greek, of which six are significantly repeated: *if* occurs four times; *also* occurs three times; *disown* occurs three times; the Greek root for *faithful* occurs three times; there are three Greek verbs which have *with* as a prefix; there are two Greek verbs with the Greek root for *remain*.

These repetitions set up the rhythmic beat of the hymn and accentuate the contrasts which populate its five lines. Although it is almost impossible to find an exact artistic match to this New Testament hymn in contemporary liturgical hymns, I offer "I Know That My Redeemer Lives" as an example of a hymn which "works" because of repetition, especially the repetition of *lives* fifteen times:

> I know that my Redeemer lives.
> What joy the blest assurance gives.
> He lives, he lives, who once was dead.
> He lives my everliving head.
>
> He lives triumphant from the grave.
> He lives eternally to save.
> He lives in majesty above.
> He lives to guide his church in love.
>
> He lives to silence all my fears.
> He lives to wipe away my tears.
> He lives to calm my troubled heart.
> He lives all blessings to impart.
>
> He lives all glory to his name.
> He lives my Savior, still the same.
> What joy this blest assurance gives.
> I know that my Redeemer lives.

Although this hymn surpasses the hymn of 2 Timothy in artistic niceties like rhyme and *inclusio* (the opening line of the hymn matches its concluding line and does so in this instance with a chiasm), it is a superb exemplar of how repetition helps create and convey a message.

My second observation deals with a more complicated level of the hymnic structure: the contrasts between the conditional sentences of lines one through four. The *if* phrases of lines one and two emphasize a positive human response to Jesus Christ whereas the *if* phrases of lines three and four underscore a negative human response to Jesus Christ. Continuing this line of analysis, I note that the second part of lines one and two proclaims a happy outcome to the positive responses given to Jesus Christ in the conduct manifested in the *if* phrases of these lines. When, however, we come to the outcome of the negative response given to Jesus Christ in the conduct manifested in the *if* phrases of lines three and four, we notice a discrepancy. Whereas line three reads "if we shall disown him, he will also disown us," line four does not follow a similar logic. That is, line four does not read "if we are unfaithful (to him), he is also unfaithful (to us)." Rather line four follows the divine logic of fidelity and trumpets: "if we are unfaithful, he remains faithful." And to make sure that readers/singers have not missed the startling message of line four, the composer has added line five: "for he cannot disown himself." One might say that the composer has set up the expectation in his listeners that the positive emphasis of lines one and two will be contrasted with the negative emphasis of lines three and four. But after meeting their expectations in line three, the composer torpedoes these self-same expectations in lines four and five. The deep meaning of this reversal of expectation will occupy our attention in the section on "Key Concepts and Images."

Almost in passing, I mention that Lucien Deiss' hymn, "Keep In Mind," has allowed many of us contemporary hymn singers to gain some appreciation of the contrasts found in 2 Timothy 2:11-13. Deiss used 2 Timothy 2:8, "Remember Jesus Christ, raised from the dead," as the basis for his song's refrain and devoted the six verses of his song to lines one and two of the Pauline hymn, thus accentuating the positive aspect of 2 Timothy 2:11-13. Perhaps another composer will incorporate all five lines of 2 Timothy 2:11-13 into a new hymn.

Clearly, 2 Timothy 2:11-13 is adorned with artistic features and thus meets one of the criteria for being considered a hymn. But we must ask whether its artistically constructed lines meet another principal criterion of a hymn which was noted in Chapter II. That is, do they sing the praises of an exalted figure? At first glance, the hymn is more about us than about Christ Jesus. At least that is the impression that lines one and two give. But when we pay serious attention to lines three through five, we quickly become aware that these three lines carry the theological weight of this "faithful" saying. That is, what is key is not what we believers accomplish (lines one and two). Rather, what is key is Christ Jesus' power to judge us at the resurrection of the dead (line three) and his fidelity to his elect (lines four and five). In other words, the hymn's celebration of our freedom as believers in lines one through three pales in comparison to the hymn's celebration of the graciousness of Christ Jesus in lines four and five. This hymn is indeed Christological.

With the above analysis I make my case that 2 Timothy 2:11-13 is indeed a hymn. I also remark that commentators are almost unanimous in holding the same opinion. See, for example, what A. T. Hanson writes: "The four lines that follow in vv. 11b-13a are undoubtedly a quotation from an early Christian hymn" (1982, 132). Given this dominant opinion among commentators and the fact that this hymn is deeply Christological, it is amazing that authors like Jack T. Sanders and Ben Witherington III have not included it in their treatment of *the* New Testament Christological hymns. Perhaps these scholars omit this hymn from their list because it does not stem from the wisdom background which they favor as the cardinal background for interpreting Christological hymns. Interested readers may consult my chapter, "Let's Do a Background Check," for more details about the studies of Sanders and Witherington.

B. THE CONTEXT

The *immediate* context of the hymn gives us a clear indication of how the author wants us to interpret its five lines. In 2 Timothy 2:8-10, Paul is presented as one who is suffering for the gospel and *remaining steadfast* in his tribulations: "Remember Jesus Christ, raised from the dead, a descendent of David: such is my gospel, for which I am suffering, even to the point of chains, like a criminal. But the word of God is not chained. Therefore, I *remain steadfast* in everything for the sake of those who are chosen, so that they too may obtain the salvation that is in Christ Jesus, together with eternal glory." Although this exhortation is addressed to the Church leader Timothy, its audience is much larger and encompasses all those who are suffering for their faith in Christ Jesus. In other words, the hymn offers consolation and hope to all those who *remain steadfast* (see line two of the hymn) during their battles for and over the faith.

Verses which immediately follow the hymn provide another significant context for its interpretation. The hymn is being cited against those who maintain that the general resurrection has already occurred: "Avoid profane, idle talk, for such people will become more and more godless, and their teaching will spread like gangrene. Among them are Hymenaeus and Philetus, who have deviated from the truth by saying that *the resurrection has already taken place* and are upsetting the faith of some" (2 Tim 2:16-18; emphasis mine). The author utilizes the hymn to make it very clear that the general resurrection has not happened. See the future tenses of the two verbs in the main clauses of the conditional sentences of lines one and two: "If we have died with him, we *shall* also live with him; if we remain steadfast, we *shall* also reign with him" (emphasis mine). That is, the life of the general resurrection remains future. It is erroneous to say that it has already taken place.

Philip Towner is correct in showing how the author of the Pastoral Epistles has drawn yet another lesson from the hymn to argue against the tenets of the opponents mentioned in 2 Timothy 2:16-18. Line two of the hymn clearly declares that Christian existence, or "remaining steadfast," is not yet completed and "by its nature requires an appropriate and sustained human response. In the midst of apostasy, the readers could not fail to understand that the decision to deny Christ, by teaching or adhering to false doctrine, is one that carries dire consequences—denial by Christ" (1989, 107).

The *broader context* of the Pastoral Epistles sheds further light on how the author wants us to interpret the hymn. 2 Timothy, which has been rightly called Paul's last will and testament, contains many references to Paul's sufferings. See 2 Timothy 1:8,12; 3:11-12; 4:6-8,18. 2 Timothy 4:6-8 is particularly enlightening as it indicates that the author has chosen to leave as a testament for the Pauline churches a portrait of Paul as the *suffering* apostle. And this legacy is not only for church leaders, but for all believers: "For I am already being poured out like a libation, and the time of my departure is at hand. I have competed well; I have finished the race; I have kept the faith. From now on *the crown of righteousness* awaits me, which the Lord, the just judge, will award to me on that day, and not only to me, but to all who have longed for his appearance" (emphasis mine). What better commentary could one want for line two of our hymn: "If we remain steadfast, we shall also reign with him."

1 Timothy 4:1-5 also shines a brilliant light on the meaning of the heretics' teaching that "the resurrection has already taken place" (2 Timothy 2:18). In 1 Timothy 4:1-5, Paul takes theological issue with the opponents' teachings that creation is not good, that marriage is forbidden, and abstinence from certain foods is mandatory. With their distrust and hatred of material creation, it is not surprising that the opponents deny the resurrection of the body and teach that resurrection is the elevation of the immaterial or spiritual part of human beings in ecstasy. And such ecstasy has already taken place and has lifted the heretics above and out of their evil, material bodies. Against such a position the hymn of 2 Timothy 2:11-13 reinforces the necessity of working out one's salvation in the here and now of bodily life.

A final interpretive element in the broader context consists of the other "faithful sayings" in the Pastoral Epistles. (See 1 Tim 1:15; 1 Tim 2:15–3:1; 1 Tim 4:9-10; Titus 3:4-8.) Titus 3:4-7 is similar to 2 Timothy 2:11-13 because it is a hymn and has a number of lines. I have devoted a chapter in this book to a study of the hymn in Titus 3:4-7. 1 Timothy 1:15 and 1 Timothy 4:9-10, being short in length, are not hymns, but contain creedal formulations. I am of the opinion that the "faithful" saying of 1 Timothy 3:1 actually refers back to the author's teaching in 2:15 about the goodness of the marriage act, conception, and childbearing, in contrast to the negative opinion of such material things held by the opponents. To the author of the Pastoral Epistles the "faithful" sayings command the response of faith from their auditors and give believers the secure comfort of keeping in mind during difficult times a clear and crisp formulation of Christian truth.

In brief, the immediate and broader contexts of the hymn of 2 Timothy 2:11-13 show how the author has interpreted what the hymn says about Christian existence and the Christian's ultimate dependence on Christ Jesus. In what follows I will try to reveal other layers of meaning in the five lines which constitute this hymn.

C. KEY CONCEPTS AND IMAGES

The immediate and broader contexts of the Pastoral Epistles have predisposed us to interpret the hymn of 2 Timothy 2:11-13 as (1) an exhortation to Christians to remain steadfast in faith in the midst of sufferings for the gospel; and (2) as a refutation of those heretics who maintain that the general resurrection has already occurred. In what follows I offer a somewhat different understanding of the hymn, one which tries to capture what it might have meant outside of its present context. The heading of this chapter conveys my understanding: We Sinners Can Depend on Jesus at the Last Judgment. I proceed in two stages.

My first stage deals with the fact that many commentators view the hymn of 2 Timothy 2:11-13 as baptismal. Their main evidence is found in line one: "For if we have died with him, we shall also live with him." This conditional sentence is very similar to Romans 6:8, which occurs in Paul's lengthy discussion about baptism: "If, then, we have died with Christ, we believe that we shall also live with him."

While it is clear that the composer draws upon Paul's discussion of the Christian baptism as a basis for his opening line, it is not clear that, by citing Romans 6:8, the composer wants his readers to read into line one all of Paul's theology of baptism as found in Romans 6:2-23. From the composer's emphasis on "remaining steadfast" in line two, I would judge that the composer agrees with at least this much of Romans 6:2-23: Paul's insistence that the battle against sin is continuous and requires that the baptized be always ready for combat. See, for example, Romans 6:13: "And do not present the parts of your bodies to sin as weapons for wickedness, but present yourselves to God as raised from the dead to life and the parts of your bodies to God as weapons for righteousness."

Lines three and four, with their inclusion of "disown" and "unfaithful," also seem to affirm the baptismal nature of the hymn of 2 Timothy 2:11-13. Such language implies a relationship of commitment and loyalty on a profound level. And the ritual of baptism seems to be the occasion for initiation into such a personal commitment and loyalty to Jesus Christ. That is, we are not talking about the level of loyalty that might exist between employee and employer. Rather we are talking about a commitment analogous to that which a husband and wife make at their wedding or to that between parents and children. In this context, think of the stories you have heard of parents disowning their children because the children joined a different faith or did some dastardly deed.

Such are the arguments for viewing 2 Timothy 2:11-13 as a baptismal hymn. It would be beneficial for readers to compare this hymn's understanding of baptism with that found in the hymns of Titus 3:4-7 and 1 Peter 3:18-22, hymns which are discussed in other chapters of this book. But for the present, we leave this discussion to take a look at my second point.

Consider the vision of the future opened up by lines two through five of our hymn. I proceed line by line. In my earlier observations in this chapter I presented much material about how the immediate and broader contexts have interpreted the meaning of "remaining steadfast" in line two. I only need to make two additional comments at this juncture. First, it is obvious the composer does not believe that the future of living and reigning with Jesus Christ (lines one and two) will arrive automatically. We Christians must continue to die to sin (line one) and remain steadfast (line two). Such is our response to God's graciousness.

Second, there are two New Testament passages which help us to interpret the promise of reward for steadfastness in suffering found in line two. One potent interpretive parallel is Romans 8:16-17: "The Spirit itself bears witness with our spirit that we are children of God, and if children, then heirs, heirs of God and joint heirs with Christ, if only we suffer with him so that we may also be glorified with him." For Paul, the Spirit given in baptism enables Christians to suffer with Christ in a steadfast manner and to be glorified with Christ. The second helpful parallel is Luke 21:19, where Jesus encourages his disciples as he forewarns them that they will suffer persecution because of their faith in him: "By remaining steadfast you will secure your lives." These parallels indicate that line two not only has present perseverance in mind, but also the Christian's future sharing in Jesus' glory. Put another way, line two (and line one), while focusing on baptism, is also looking to the future life and rule with Jesus.

Line three joins lines one and two in focusing the Christians' attention on the future. Along with most commentators, I think that Matthew 10:33 lies at the base of line three: "Whoever disowns me before others, I will also disown before my heavenly Father." Again as with Luke 21:19, the situation envisaged in Matthew 10:26-33 is one in which the disciples are persecuted because of their commitment to Jesus. In order to put Matthew 10:33 into even greater perspective it is helpful to quote its positive parallel in the verse which precedes it: "Everyone who acknowledges me before others I will acknowledge before my heavenly Father" (Matt 10:32).

So much for an interpretive parallel for line three. What does line three mean for Christians who know that they have sinned against their baptismal commitment? It seems to me that commentators begin to earn their keep as they struggle to interpret line three (and lines four and five as well) in light of this question, for such a concern is literally a matter of life and death for both the commentators and those who are nurtured by their teaching.

I agree with many commentators who interpret the "when" of line three by means of the parallel of Matthew 10:33. That is, Jesus will disown at the last judgment those who disown him. But it is unclear whether the future tense of the *if* clause also refers to the last judgment. Does "if we shall disown him" refer to a person's definitive intention in the presence of Jesus Christ as judge? Or does it refer to apostasy from Jesus any time after baptism but before the last judgment, therefore allowing time for the baptized Christian to repent before the final judgment? Whichever interpretation is accepted, it is clear either way that disowning Jesus Christ has dire consequences for their future life.

It seems best to me to follow those commentators who formulate the question of lines four and five this way: Do these lines convey threat or promise? It is the position of a few commentators that line four emphasizes Jesus' fidelity to his resolve to disown those who have been baptized and have disowned him and have been unfaithful to him. If Jesus would not disown them, he would be unfaithful and would actually disown his very nature (line five). This is the *threat* position and is to be congratulated for emphasizing the heinous nature of the baptized's betrayal of Jesus Christ. But scholars rightfully challenge this position because it makes the composer take an extra two lines (four and five) to say what the composer had already said in line three. Put in artistic terms, this position maintains that the composer who displayed great skill in authoring lines one through three lost his skill in the writing of lines four and five and resorted to circumlocutions and fruitless paradox.

While finding the *threat* position inadequate, I approach the *promise* position with a paeon of alleluias and also with much fear and trembling because it is almost too good to be true, especially in the light of the many times Christians have acted contrary to their baptismal commitment to Jesus Christ. In my opinion the key passage for interpreting the profound meaning of lines four and five comes from Romans, an epistle which has figured frequently in our previous analyses of this hymn. In Romans 3:3 Paul picks up a thread of his argument, that God has not abandoned God's promised people, the Jews, even though some have been unfaithful. He writes: "What if some were unfaithful? Will their infidelity nullify the fidelity of God?" In another passage where he does not use the terminology of faithfulness, Paul alludes to the same reality when he writes of God's dealing with the Jewish people: "For the gifts and the call of God are irrevocable" (11:29).

What enlightenment does Romans 3:3 and 11:29 bring to lines four and five? Plenty! The *if* clauses of lines one through four have stressed the power of human free will, with positive results in lines one and two and with negative results in lines three and four. But as the main clause of line four and all of line five proclaim, one's life with Jesus Christ is not totally dependent on human free will. The salvation of each and every baptized person is dependent on the fidelity of Jesus Christ to his part of the commitment sealed in baptism. Yes, commitment is a two-way street. Let Christians who glory in their exalted notions of their own free will never forget that point. In the points for reflection which follow I will pursue this analysis further. At this point it seems good to quote from a few representative commentators on lines four and five, lest my readers think that I have overdosed on God's mercy and become oblivious to God's righteous punishment of sin.

Representative of the British commentators is J.N.D. Kelly: "This does not mean, 'God keeps his word both for reward and for punishment' (W. Lock), i.e., relentlessly exacts the penalty due to our backsliding. The great affirmation of the hymn is that, however wayward and faithless men may be, God's love continues unalterable and he remains true to his promises. . . . To be faithful through everything, in spite of the worst that men can do, is the essence of his nature" (1963, 180–81).

The North American representative commentator is Gordon D. Fee. Apropos of line four, Fee writes: ". . . sharp differences of opinion exist regarding its interpretation. Some see it as a negative . . . God must be faithful to himself and mete out judgment. Although such an understanding is possible, it seems highly improbable. . . . After all, that could have been said plainly. The lack of a future verb with the adverb 'also,' as well as the fact that God's faithfulness in the NT is always in behalf of his people, also tend to speak out against this view" (1984, 250–51). And concerning line five Fee opines: "Hence eschatological salvation is for Paul ultimately rooted in the character of God" (1984, 254).

In conclusion to this section, I recall my heading for this chapter: "We Sinners Can Depend on Jesus at the Last Judgment." Because of Jesus' fidelity, reliability, and dependability, the future does indeed look bright for Christian sinners. In dealing with baptism and a faithful Christian life, the hymn holds the future of Jesus' last judgment firmly in view. The hymn does not utilize the apocalyptic props of an archangel's voice or a trumpet's blast (1 Thess 4:16) nor the apocalyptic scenario of the separation of sheep and goats (Matt 25:31-46) to describe the final judgment. Rather the hymn casts brilliant light on the main character in this eschatological drama—Jesus Christ who manifests God's ultimate fidelity to those who are called.

D. Reflection Starters

I will use the image of journey for my reflections upon what the hymn of 2 Timothy 2:11-13 might say about spirituality. I view our hymn from three basic contextual perspectives.

First, from the immediate and broader contexts of the Pastoral Epistles as well as from personal experience, we realize that the journey of faith will involve suffering for the faith. Perhaps such suffering does not occur very frequently in most parts of North America today and its possibility may be so remote that reflection upon exhortations to "remain steadfast" in the face of adversity may seem irrelevant. But what if we turn to other areas of the world where members of Christ's body may be suffering for the faith or have just emerged from such troubles?

A short time ago my work brought me to Lithuania, one of the Baltic States which had been under atheistic communist rule for fifty years. When I asked my hosts how the people had been able to maintain their faith in such circumstances, they told me horror stories about how the KGB had severely punished people who went to church "too often," or who had a church wedding, or who had their children baptized. Amidst such brutality, many people gave up the practices of their faith. And these stories took on faces when I was introduced to a catechist who had spent fourteen years in prison for merely teaching religion to children. When I was introduced to clergy, very often I heard the formula: This is Father *X*, who spent *Y* number of years in Siberia for the faith. In such a situation of great suffering for the faith, I think that lines four and five of our hymn are especially pertinent: "If we are unfaithful, Jesus Christ remains faithful, for he cannot deny himself." And with regard to the persecutors, the contemporary Church in Lithuania challenges itself with Jesus' message from his Sermon on the Mount: forgive your enemies and be reconciled to them. In summary, at times when Christians must endure great suffering to remain steadfast in their faith, we realize that we may not be in charge of our journey of faith, for forces far greater than us are shoving us off the road and disabling us. During those times, our prayer—and that of our fellow believers—stems from profound trust in the fidelity of Jesus Christ who has called us.

Second, the context of the Pastoral Epistles has cautioned us about those opponents of the faith who deny the future resurrection and thus deprive us baptized Christians of the goal of our journey and cheapen our daily struggles and joys in the body as if they were of no account. These opponents don't want us to enjoy music and sing hymns, to fall in love and form lasting friendships, to smack our lips over juicy blood-red Sicilian oranges, or to drink pleasurable potions. These heretics have disowned Christ, are upsetting the community of faith, and, as line three of the hymn declares, will suffer the consequences of their actions in the future at the last judgment when Christ disowns those who continue to disown him. Yet the context of the Pastoral Epistles, especially Titus 3:10-11, does not fully reckon with lines four and five: Jesus Christ is in charge of our journey of faith and is faithful to those who are called. That is, the hymn itself may display more brilliantly God's graciously forgiving countenance to both wholehearted and halfhearted travelers on faith's journey than the author of the Pastoral Epistles does.

Third, I have interpreted 2 Timothy 2:11-13 against the background of New Testament writings like Romans. Perhaps we can use the context of those New Testament passages to tease out some additional insights for a spirituality of journey.

While free will is important for those who have been baptized into Christ and have embarked on the journey of faith, we should not see it as the only companion we take on the journey. This is a hard lesson for us North Americans to accept, for we breathe the air of rank individualism and have been raised on a diet of *me first*. Although free will is vitally important on our journey of faith, it is not the only odometer available to measure our progress. The emphasis on human free will in the *if* clauses of lines one through four must be contrasted with what is said about the fidelity of our Savior Jesus Christ in lines four and five. Jesus Christ is not only our judge at the last judgment. Jesus Christ is also our dependable companion on our journey to be *with* him. Although we may be unfaithful to our baptismal commitment to Jesus, Jesus remains faithful to us. And lines three through five can surely bear the theological insight that even if the baptized should ever disown Christ by apostasy and abandon the journey of faith, their future remains one of hope until they make their apostasy definitive at the last judgment.

I end my reflections on a number of notes, and begin by acknowledging that I have devoted many pages to the much neglected and hope-inspiring hymn found in 2 Timothy 2:11-13 and have included it under the category of hymns which deal with the theme of the future God has in store for believers. For those who would group this hymn with Titus 3:4-7 and 1 Peter 3:18-22, hymns which feature baptism, I concede the reasonableness of choosing to do so. For interested readers, I emphasize the importance of the interpreter's task and challenge of consulting various contexts to understand a hymn. I also remind interpreters that the hymn itself may say more than its immediate and broader contexts allow it to say, e.g., about the ultimate fate of the heretics. In my chapter on Colossians 1:15-20, I present a similar hermeneutical situation. For those who have enjoyed wrestling with the theological paradox of lines four and five of 2 Timothy 2:11-13, I conclusively conclude my conclusion by quoting two prayers of Søren Kierkegaard,[1] the Danish existentialist philosopher and theologian who lived from 1813-1855 and who paraded in phrasing paradox. The songsters among you may be interested to know that the American composer Samuel Barber (1910–1981), who is best known for his "Adagio for Strings," set five of Kierkegaard's prayers to music, including the first of the two which follow:

> I. Father in Heaven!
> Do not hold our sins up against us
> But hold us up against our sins,
> So that the thought of you,
> When it wakens in our soul,
> And each time it wakens,
> Should not remind us
> Of what we have committed,
> But of what you have forgiven;
> Not of how we went astray,
> But of how you saved us.

> II. You who in our earliest childhood received our promise,
> You to whom at baptism we gave our promise of faithfulness,
> Father in heaven, grant
> That throughout our life we do not forget our promise, our commitment,
> That we do not forget to come to your wedding,
> Whatever excuses we might find.
> These pretexts are indifferent things;
> The decisive thing for us would be that we didn't come to the wedding.

---

[1]These prayers are adapted from *The Prayers of Kierkegaard Edited and with a New Interpretation of His Life and Thought* by Perry D. LeFevre (Chicago: University of Chicago Press, 1956) 21, 35.

ANNOTATED BIBLIOGRAPHY

Fee, Gordon D. *1 and 2 Timothy, Titus.* New International Biblical Commentary. Peabody: Hendrickson, 1984. In this helpful commentary, Fee champions the view that Paul wrote the Pastoral Epistles.

Hanson, A. T. *The Pastoral Epistles.* New Century Bible Commentary. Grand Rapids: Eerdmans, 1982. A solid treatment of these three often neglected letters from the perspective that Paul did not author them.

Kelly, J.N.D. *A Commentary on The Pastoral Epistles.* Black's New Testament Commentaries. London: Adam & Charles Clark, 1963. This early Church scholar holds that Paul wrote 1 and 2 Timothy and Titus.

Towner, Philip H. *The Goal of Our Instruction: The Structure of Theology and Ethics in the Pastoral Epistles.* Journal for the Study of the New Testament Supplement Series 34. Sheffield: JSOT Press, 1989. The outstanding value of this monograph is that it moves beyond the decades-old debate of whether Paul wrote the Pastoral Epistles and looks more fruitfully at the author's theological and ethical horizons.

N.B. Interested readers will find additional bibliography in the chapters dealing with the hymns of 1 Timothy 3:16 and Titus 3:4-7.

IX. CONCLUSION

As we come to the end of the Karris Symphony, I deem it wise to recapitulate its major themes and propose areas for further exploration.

A strong motif in my symphony has been *context,* a point generally underplayed in studies of New Testament hymns. In discussing each hymn, I have emphasized the significance of the hymn's immediate and broader context. In certain chapters I have also interpreted a hymn, e.g., Titus 3:4-7, within the larger context of Paul's letters. At times I have called my reader's attention to what happens to a hymn when it is set within a particular liturgical context, e.g., Philippians 2:6-11. In my discussions of Colossians 1:15-20 and 2 Timothy 2:11-13, I suggested that the author of the hymn had a different (and more theologically sound?) understanding of God and God's ways than the author of the epistle in which the hymn is found. The interested reader might want to ask: Is there any hymn in the New Testament whose meaning is conveyed straightaway, that is, without a context?

I have also emphasized the role of *traditions.* The New Testament hymns are traditions which predate the letters in which they appear. Some hymns, e.g., Philippians 2:6-11, may have been composed a mere ten years after Jesus' crucifixion. But all, I would surmise, were written before or shortly after 60 C.E. It seems to me that the process of incorporating traditions into New Testament letters needs to be studied with greater intensity. For example, it is now quite clear that Paul used many and diverse traditions, e.g., Romans 1:3-4, when composing what some scholars call his Big Seven epistles: Romans, 1 and 2 Corinthians, Galatians, Philippians, 1 Thessalonians, and Philemon. It is worth asking to what

extent Paul's use of traditions differed from that of the authors of
the deutero-Pauline letters, five of whose hymns we have studied
in this book. On a larger front, to what extent does the epistolary
use of traditions differ from or accord with the use of traditions on
the part of the evangelists? More particularly, does the author of
Colossians use Wisdom traditions in 1:15-20 the same way that
the Fourth Evangelist does in the Prologue?

From time to time I have also emphasized the role and importance of *ambiguity* in the hymns we discussed. Recall, for example, my discussion of the meanings of "the wall" in Ephesians
2:14-16 or of the meanings of "preached to the spirits in prison"
in 1 Peter 3:19. I further remind my readers that ambiguity is
something positive in hymns and poems. If I momentarily abandon the term "ambiguity," which may have some negative conno-
tations in North American society, I willingly adapt expressions
from the study of interpretation (hermeneutics): "pluriformity of
meaning" or "surplus of meaning." Thus, the symbol "the wall" in
Ephesians 2:14-16 has plural meanings, even an abundance or
surplus of meaning beyond the immediate reference to something
material which blocks my passage. So, too, does "buckle" have
multiple meanings in Gerard Manley Hopkins' sonnet, "The
Windhover" (see my chapter on Colossians 1:15-20).

Although no summary will do justice to the total content of all
seven hymns we have investigated, I will provide some sense of
their common elements, especially their emphases (1) on Christ as
universal Lord, who (2) was human to the point of crucifixion and
(3) has defeated the Powers. I leave it to interested readers to make
still more exact determinations of these three common elements.

In their own ways the hymns of Ephesians 2:14-16, Colossians
1:15-20, 1 Timothy 3:16, and 1 Peter 3:18-22 proclaim what
Philippians 2:9-11 does so emphatically and expansively: "Wherefore God highly exalted him and bestowed upon him the name
which is above every name, so that at the name of Jesus every
knee should bend of those in heaven, on earth, and under the
earth; and every tongue should confess that Jesus Christ is LORD
to the glory of God the Father." Verily, Jesus Christ is Lord of all.

Each and every hymn weds this exalted Lord Jesus Christ to
human history. As I quote from our seven hymns, I ask my read-

ers to note how often Jesus Christ's human history is specified by his death by crucifixion:

Philippians 2:8:	"death on a cross"
Ephesians 2:14:	"through his flesh"
Ephesians 2:16:	"through his cross"
Colossians 1:18:	"firstborn from the dead"
Colossians 1:20:	"blood of his cross"
1 Timothy 3:16:	"in the flesh"
2 Timothy 2:11:	"if we have died with him"
Titus 3:4:	"appeared"
1 Peter 3:18:	"put to death in the flesh"

The same five hymns I listed under "Jesus Christ is Lord of all" return to our stage under the category "the Lord has defeated the Powers":

Philippians 2:10:	"every knee should bend, of those in heaven and on earth and under the earth"
Ephesians 2:14:	"tore down the dividing wall of hostility"
Colossians 1:20:	"and through him to reconcile all things for him, making peace through the blood of his cross, through him, whether those on earth or those in heaven"
1 Timothy 3:16:	"revealed to the angels"
1 Peter 3:19:	"In it he also went to preach to the spirits in prison."

It is somewhat easy to comb through our seven hymns and find their common elements. And although my readers might quibble about whether one of the three common elements is present in a particular hymn, they would generally agree with my summary.

We begin a more difficult and controverted analysis, however, when we return to one of the questions of chapter one—*Whence* these common elements? Of course, it is easy to determine that the common element of Jesus Christ's humanity came from the fact that Christ was human, and indeed was crucified. But what is the source of the other two common elements?

In chapter two I whetted your appetite for more information about the origins of the common elements of Jesus Christ as Lord of all and conqueror of the Powers by mentioning the role of the

Holy Spirit, the early Christians' deep religious experiences, theological antecedents in the Wisdom literature, especially Proverbs and the Wisdom of Solomon, and a long tradition of diverse hymn making in Judaism. Here I want to elaborate on two of those "origins," thus engaging in what I called "synthetic parallelism" in chapter one. Interested readers might want to note that this type of "synthetic parallelism" is also called *inclusio,* as at the end I return to and include thoughts first articulated at the beginning.

The monograph of Larry W. Hurtado (1988) has been singularly helpful in showing that in addition to the divine agent "wisdom," Jewish thinkers also theologized about two other divine agents as they grappled with God's dealings with the world. They reflected upon the divine agents of "exalted patriarchs" like Enoch and Moses and the divine agents of "principal angels" like Daniel, Michael, and Raphael. According to Hurtado the Jewish category of "divine agency" provided the earliest Christians with the conceptual framework needed to explain Jesus' exaltation to God's "right hand" (1988, 12). That is, the earliest Jewish Christians could more readily proclaim that God had exalted Jesus to the position of glory at God's right hand because they were used to placing other exalted figures in this supreme position, namely, Wisdom and Enoch and Michael.

In my foundational chapter I also mentioned the role of Christian experience in the formulation of the first Christian hymns. Building upon Hurtado's work, I would like to suggest that such experiences were the events which the earliest Christians tried to explain by means of the category of "divine agency." Accompany me in your religious imagination as we eavesdrop on a very early Christian prayer gathering. Somewhere through the hours-long ceremony of music, Eucharistic eating together, and sharing of faith you and I and our fellow Christians have an experience of the glory of Jesus Christ. Such a profound experience calls for an explanation. How is the crucified Jesus now in such glory, indeed, at God's right hand? Isn't he like Wisdom, who was with God at the very beginning? Isn't he like Enoch who was taken up to God? Isn't he like the principal angel Michael? But whereas no one in Judaism singled out Wisdom or Enoch or Michael for devotion, veneration, indeed, worship, you and your fellow Christians proclaim that Jesus is not only Lord, but *your* Lord.

As Hurtado writes: "It is more likely that the initial and main reason that this particular chief agent (Jesus) came to share in the religious devotion of this particular Jewish group (the earliest Christians) is that they had visions and other experiences that communicated the risen and exalted Christ and that presented him in such unprecedented and superlative divine glory that they felt compelled to respond devotionally as they did" (1988, 121).

Let me develop Hurtado's points by introducing the larger Hellenistic cultural context, in which the earliest Christians made their confession of Jesus as Lord. When the Christians professed and sang that Jesus was exalted at God's right hand, they were making a conscious decision that their Lord was Christ and not Zeus or Isis. In terms of one of the broad thematics of this book the Christians were declaring that they had (1) need for an all-powerful, universal God, who (2) conquers fate and other hostile powers in an "age of anxiety." Let me add greater specificity to this component of my answer to the question Whence? by quoting from Cleanthes and Apuleius.

The Stoic philosopher Cleanthes lived from ca. 331–232 B.C.E. Among the fragments of his writings is one called "Hymn to Zeus." This hymn, which was very popular, gives evidence of the longings of Hellenistic peoples and might be profitably compared and contrasted with our New Testament hymns:

> You, O Zeus, are praised above all gods; many are your names and yours is all power for ever.
> The beginning of the world was from you: and with law you rule over all things.
> Unto you may all flesh speak: for we are your offspring.
> Therefore will I raise a hymn unto you: and will ever sing of your power.
> The whole order of the heavens obeys your word: as it moves around the earth.
> With little and great lights mixed together: how great are you, King above all for ever.
> Nor is anything done upon earth apart from you: nor in the firmament, nor in the seas:
> Save that which the wicked do: by their own folly.
> But yours is the skill to set even the crooked straight: what is without fashion is fashioned and the alien akin before you.

> Thus have you fitted together all things in one: the good with the
>   evil:
> That your word should be one in all things: abiding for ever.
> Let folly be dispersed from our souls: that we may repay you the
>   honor, wherewith you have honored us:
> Singing praise of your works forever: as become the sons of men
>   (Barrett 1989, 67 modified).

If Zeus were to be god, Zeus had to be universal, e.g., ruling over all things. In a milieu in which the "Hymn to Zeus" was sung, would-be converts to Christianity, be they Jewish or Gentile, had to be assured and had to experience in conscious faith that the crucified Jesus was universal Lord.

At the time when the New Testament hymns were composed, mystery religions were on the rise. Granted that they were primarily the fare of the rich because of the cost of their initiation rites and granted further that they did not deal with historical persons, nevertheless they proclaimed a god or goddess who was universal savior. I bring to my reader's attention the most popular of saviors in the first century C.E. Her name was Isis, whose clients sang her praises in what scholars call an "aretalogy" or litany of virtues. I quote from Lucius' aretalogy of Isis in Apuleius' *The Golden Ass* xi:

> O holy and blessed Lady, the perpetual comfort of humankind, who by your bounty and grace nourish all the world, and bear a great affection to the adversities of the miserable as a loving mother, you take no rest night or day, neither are you idle at any time in giving benefits and succouring all men as well on land as sea; you are she that put away all storms and dangers from men's life by stretching forth your right hand, whereby likewise you do unweave even the inextricable and tangled web of fate, and appease the great tempests of forture, and keep back the harmful course of the stars. The gods supernal do honor you; the gods infernal have you in reverence; you make all the earth to turn, you give light to the sun, you govern the world, you tread down the power of hell. By your mean the stars give answer, the seasons return, the gods rejoice, the elements serve: at your command the winds do blow, the clouds nourish the earth, the seeds prosper, and the fruits do grow. The birds of the air, the beasts of the hill, the serpents of the den, and the fishes of the sea do tremble at your majesty (Barrett 1989, 128–29 modified).

From this "aretalogy" it is surely clear that Isis is in charge of all things, even "fate" and "the great tempests of fortune." Those who are burdened and needful of salvation are invited by the singers of her "aretalogy" to hasten to her for help. Philippians 2:6-11, Ephesians 2:14-16, Colossians 1:15-20, 1 Timothy 3:16, and 1 Peter 3:18-22 make it very clear that Jesus Christ, and not Isis, is Lord, that Jesus Christ has conquered fate and every conceivable power that might separate any believer from God. That is, the Christians who faithfully sing these hymns announce to one and all that the crucified Jesus is not only their Wisdom, exalted to God's right hand like Enoch and living with God like Archangel Michael, but also mightier than Isis.

Cleanthes "Hymn to Zeus" and Lucius "Aretalogy of Isis" give us sufficient evidence of the larger Hellenistic philosophical and religious context in which New Testament hymns were composed. On one level, these philosophical and religious texts demonstrate the longings of Hellenistic peoples for a savior, who is powerful enough to be Lord of everything, fate included. The New Testament hymns also respond to these longings of people living in an "age of anxiety." On another level, these texts give evidence of the "universalist thrust" of philosophical and religious discourse as it seeks to transcend the pedestrian categories of language and talk about universal and all-embracing truth. And what is most amazing of all is that our hymns find universal truth in One who manifested God through a human life, even to death by crucifixion.

In this context the observations of Elisabeth Schüssler Fiorenza are right on target: ". . . the early Christian hymns speak of Jesus Christ in mythological language in order to emphasize his universal importance. . . . Both hymns (Phil 2:6-11; 1 Tim 3:16) are interested in proclaiming the universal and cosmic rulership of Christ as *the kyrios*. They attempt therefore to show, each in a different way, that Jesus Christ is not only equal but superior to all the gods and lords of the Greco-Roman world and that he is acknowledged as such not only by the Christians but by the whole world. The mythological language which they employ can not be derived from a single basic myth or from a developing redeemer myth. Instead, as in Jewish-Hellenistic wisdom speculation, this mythological language is probably developed in dialogue with various mythic beliefs and thought-contexts of the time" (1975, 37–38). Interested readers will find corroboration for Schüssler Fiorenza's explanation for the universalist dimension of New Testament hymns from Pheme Perkins, whose work on Gnosticism I cited in my chapter on backgrounds. I also invite interested readers to refer back to the end of my chapter on 1 Timothy 3:16 for my views on the pursuit of truth undertaken by mythopoeic thinking and remind them that Christian myth is not falsehood. Rather, it is a truth-filled narrative whose symbols lead us readers and believers up a road to encounter the crucified, risen, and victorious Jesus Christ, our Lord.

So there you have it. A summary of what nine chapters have said about the contexts of our hymns, their traditional character, their common elements, and their possible sources in Jewish thinking about divine agency, in Hellenistic philosophical and religious thought and expectations, and in Christian religious experience of the crucified Jesus Christ as exalted to God's right hand. Obviously, there's plenty of work still to be done on New Testament hymns, perhaps even by the present composer in his Second Symphony. But sufficient for the day is this repertoire of hymns and answers to this battery of questions.

As I end this book, I can only stand back in wonderment. Wonderment at the early Christians' depth of faith in Christ Jesus as Lord of all. Wonderment at how they came to believe so rapidly and so profoundly. Wonderment, too, that it has taken me twenty-five years to write this book! For in a real sense this book took its first breath in 1971 when I began my study of traditions in the New Testament with my Harvard doctoral thesis on the exhortatory and polemical traditions in the Pastoral Epistles. Through fifteen years of teaching courses on Pauline Literature at Catholic Theological Union at Chicago I broadened that study. And now that I work in a cross-cultural situation in Rome, North America, England, Ireland, and Malta I have become more keenly aware of how contexts interpret traditions, specifically, traditions about St. Francis and St. Clare of Assisi. Add to that loves for reading, writing, research, and music. Mix in the freedom to find and to take advantage of the soft spots in schedules, and you have my Symphony.

May the Karris Symphony benefit both your mind and spirit. And may you find as much delight in its reading as I have found in its composing!

ANNOTATED BIBLIOGRAPHY

Barrett, C. K. *The New Testament Background: Selected Documents.* Rev. ed. San Francisco: HarperSanFrancisco, 1989. An excellent collection of background material for interpreting New Testament hymns.

Hurtado, Larry W. *One God, One Lord: Early Christian Devotion and Ancient Jewish Monotheism.* Philadelphia: Fortress, 1988. A creative and insightful work about the Jewish background which may have been the catalyst for the early Christians' rapid belief in and devotion to Jesus Christ as their Lord.

Schüssler Fiorenza, Elisabeth. "Wisdom Mythology and the Christological Hymns of the New Testament." *Aspects of Wisdom in Judaism and Early Christianity.* Ed. Robert L. Wilken, 17–41. Notre Dame: University of Notre Dame Press, 1975. A pioneering study. Interested readers should consult the Annotated Bibliography of my chapter on Backgrounds for more details about the differing views of Schüssler Fiorenza and Jack T. Sanders about wisdom, myth, and "the Christological hymns" of the New Testament.